GOD BLESS the SICK and AFFLICTED

GOD BLESS
the SICK and
AFFLICTED

Elaine Cannon

BOOKCRAFT
Salt Lake City, Utah

Library of Congress Catalog Card Number: 89-60630

ISBN 0-88494-697-5

First Printing, 1989

Printed in the United States of America

To all the good people who have helped make this publication possible: to Sharon Lewis for the germ of an idea; to Jana Erickson and Carla Cannon for artistic help; to the executive decision-makers, the layout staff, the artists, editors, printers, binders, typists, copiers; to family and fellow sufferers in the world of affliction; and, as well, to the joyful survivors who were willing to share their stories.

If thou art sorrowful, call on the Lord thy God with supplication, that your souls may be joyful.

—D&C 136:29

Contents

Preface

Across the pulpits, beside the beds, around the tables at mealtime, from the kneeling circles of families beginning a day, in holy temples, in busy hospitals, and in private places, countless good people offer the universal plea at prayer time, "O God, bless the sick and afflicted."

What a comforting thought that is, because sooner or later we all qualify to be counted among the sick and the afflicted. How good it is then, to be included in somebody's prayer!

Afflicted is an interesting word to describe a terrible state of being. Suffering an affliction brings miserable images to mind, such as boils, shingles, bankruptcy, terminal disease, miserable personal relationships, heartbreak, death, deprivation, succumbing to temptation, or being struck down by disaster through no fault of our own.

Dictionary definitions of "affliction" include such designations as torture, suffering, persistent anguish, torment that strains the powers of endurance or of self-control, extreme embarrassment, and stress of mind and body from whatever demanding cause.

Mercy!

When you are among the sick and afflicted, you probably are plagued with accompanying feelings of doubt, hopelessness, and self-pity. You need to be reassured that you are of some value, and that life is worth living. You hang on the promise that all this experience will, indeed, be for your good. You want to feel sure that God lives and cares about you, particularly at this time.

Until this current sickness or affliction is resolved or has run its course, you seek comfort, patience, strength to endure, and sustaining support. You want God's blessings. While you may know the sweet uses of adversity, when it is your turn to be among the poor, the sick, or the afflicted, prayers are a powerful force in helping you get through the siege.

There are countless choice reports of the miracles wrought in healing, of resolution and peace resulting from God's goodness as united prayers from the faithful pour out before heaven. This book reports on answered prayers, blessings, and miracles people have enjoyed. Therefore, this is a book to comfort, to bring hope to worn hearts, and to remind one of gentler, kinder times. It is a book that proves God's love for his children and that he visits them in their affliction. It will remind you how God does bless those who are sick, those who are afflicted in diverse ways.

Along with the prayers of the righteous, perhaps this collection of thoughts can help assuage your pain and enliven your own faith.

Regarding those prayers for the sick and afflicted, there are some people who when they pray, "O God, bless the sick and afflicted" include a request that they themselves may be directed by heaven to appropriately bring comfort or cure to others in their times of assaulting affliction.

What a refreshing idea!

Doing something for others is still the best way to forget your own troubles. That's when joy can come.

God bless the sick and the afflicted?

He does!

1

Be Not Afraid

Friend, be not afraid! It's a new day. Maybe today is your day for the wonderful surprises, like inimitable hyacinths coming your way. If not, plan a surprise for someone else—surely your turn will come tomorrow.

Even though you may count yourself among the sick and the afflicted, it is only *at this time*. It is not forever. Things haven't always been this maddening, tough, stressful, demanding, disappointing for you, now have they? Life is much, much more than trouble!

Such suffering as you are enduring now sows seeds of strength as well as joy in your soul. You'll learn this again this round, sooner or later.

You know that we are expected to be examples of the believer. One of the chief opportunities and obligations of a disciple of Christ is to behave as a true believer and to witness that this way of life makes a difference.

Now, because none of us copes easily and painlessly at every given moment of a season of heartbreak, it is wise to take another look often at our guidelines for living, at our articles of faith, at our counsel from prophets, at the teachings of Jesus. We look to the scriptures to bolster our own courage and direct our own actions under stress.

For example, one of the most powerful statements in scripture is found in Joshua 1:9: "Be strong and of a good courage; be not afraid, neither be thou dismayed: for the Lord thy God is with thee whithersoever thou goest."

The Lord was talking to his prophet Joshua when he said those words, but surely they are meant for us in our day. If you read that promise enough times—memorize the lines if you can, computing these true ideas into your brain —soon it will be as if God himself is talking to you and comforting you.

The echo rings through the years, too. For example, when King David was ready to turn his throne over to his son Solomon, he gave similar counsel. "And David said to Solomon his son, Be strong and of good courage, and do it: fear not, nor be dismayed: for the Lord God, even my God, will be with thee; he will not fail thee, nor forsake thee, until thou hast finished all the work for the service of the house of the Lord" (1 Chronicles 28:20).

Paul wrote to Timothy, his beloved companion in the spiritual work of the Lord, and he explained to the young man that "God hath not given us the spirit of fear; but of power, and of love, and of a sound mind" (2 Timothy 1:7). This is a motivating promise.

Joseph Smith wrote a letter to his brethren who sat in counsel with him to discuss the affairs of the Church. This letter was for the purpose of providing "information in relation to many subjects." September 6, 1846, he wrote the following lines: "Courage, brethren, and on, on to the victory! Let your hearts rejoice, and be exceedingly glad." These early servants of God had mighty problems as well as a keen awareness of their responsibility. These were very troubled times, remember? And the Prophet Joseph dared to encourage those who suffered—not only to be courageous but to *allow* (or let) their hearts rejoice. Anyway! Wonderful, isn't it?

The Lord had something to say to Emma, who also needed comfort. These times were most strenuous for her. The Church had been organized only four months, and the level of persecution had increased frighteningly. The Smiths and their helpers were almost totally in hiding. It was difficult to move the work forward, even to deal with the daily demands. Emma was frightened, of course, but her comfort came with a special revelation for her, a woman! Unusual! Wonderful! The Lord said things to Emma such as: "Murmur not . . . the office of thy calling shall be for a comfort unto my servant, Joseph Smith, Jun., thy husband, in his afflictions, with consoling words, in the spirit of meekness. And thou needest not fear, . . . Wherefore, lift up thy heart and rejoice, . . . Keep my commandments continually, and a crown of righteousness thou shalt receive." (D&C 25:4, 5, 9, 13, 15.)

These few scriptural examples impart a message for each of us. We, too, are God's children with a mission to perform here on earth. The details may be different, but there will be tough times, that's certain. However, according to God's word for all of his children, we are not alone. We have been told not to be afraid or dismayed but to be of good courage and lift up our hearts, for God is with us.

Read again about the comfort Christ gave to his servants in the early days of The Church of Jesus Christ of Latter-day Saints, because much of the content pertains to all of us. We all are his servants to a greater or lesser degree. The reference is found in the Doctrine and Covenants 68:5-6: "This is the promise of the Lord unto you, O ye my servants. Wherefore, be of good cheer, and do not fear, *for I the Lord am with you, and will stand by you*; and ye shall bear record of me, even Jesus Christ, that I am the Son of the living God, that I was, that I am, and that I am to come."

Let's think back a moment on the scripture from Joshua. God has told us not to be afraid or dismayed but to be of good courage because "the Lord thy God is with thee whithersoever thou goest." There it is, the warming reminder that we don't have to be brave all alone.

Life teaches us that when we pray for the sick and afflicted, we also are praying for ourselves. Praying and doing must go hand in hand. This is the road to survival and, at long last, to comfort.

Eleanor Roosevelt knew something about pressure, heartache, and demanding struggle. A few years ago, with members of the National Council of Women, I visited Hyde Park, New York, the Franklin D. Roosevelt estate. There we were privileged to browse through Valkyrie, the summer cottage that became Mrs. Roosevelt's fascinating personal retreat and now is a kind of private museum. While there I learned that during a particularly threatening period of life for many Americans—World War II—Mrs. Roosevelt said, "You gain strength, courage and confidence by every experience in which you really stop to look fear in the face. You are able to say to yourself, 'I lived through this horror. I can take the next thing that comes along.' "

It was during that same war, those same awful days, that Winston Churchill said he was an optimist because it didn't seem much use being anything else.

When I was growing up, it was the thing to do around our house to clip quotes, poetry, words of wisdom, and articles of inspiration from the new slick magazines and Church periodicals. In those days I didn't understand the importance of recording proper information for future reference, but surely that doesn't change the value of the following lines attributed to Anonymous.

What is courage?
Courage is not just
To bare one's bosom to the sabre-thrust
Alone, in the daring.

Courage is to grieve,
To have the hurt, and make
The world believe
You are not caring.

Courage does not lie
Alone in dying for a cause.
To die
Is only giving.

Courage is to feel
The daily daggers
Of relentless steel
And keep on living.

Actor Jimmy Stewart has often shared the details of a particularly frightening time in his life. It was a turning point. It, too, happened during World War II. He was a squadron commander with the U.S. Eighth Air Force stationed in England. They flew huge four-engine bombers over enemy territory.

One night he was brooding about the men who hadn't come back from the day's mission and wondering who would be the ones picked off tomorrow when they would go forth again. Imagination can break a man's heart with fear and longing. It can bathe him in sweat.

Besides praying, pilot Stewart did what a capable person does under such demands—he checked and double-checked his lists. (Is there a mother in the early stages of labor, a man facing his own battle of frightening surgery, who doesn't get life in order—just in case? We'll call it preparedness instead of lack of faith.)

Then Stewart took out a worn piece of paper and lovingly unfolded it one more time. It was a letter of love and encouragement from his father, who had been through some wars of his own. He understood and had included in the letter lines from Psalm 91. Stewart felt better as he drew close to his own father in love and to Heavenly Father in increased faith.

During an interview some years later Mr. Stewart said, "I had no illusions about the mission that was coming up. I knew very well what might happen. And I knew that fear would ride with me. But I would live with it—and almost welcome it. Because, in its proper place, it would be an asset, sharpening perceptions, simplifying skills, and heightening the capacity for quick decisions. I had done all I could. I had faced each fear and handed it over to God . . . and I knew that He would be with me in this world or the next."

Read again these strengthening words included in the ninety-first Psalm. Surely they will help you be unafraid: "I will say of the Lord, He is my refuge and my fortress: my God; in him will I trust. . . . Because thou hast made the Lord, . . . my refuge, . . . There shall no evil befall thee, neither shall any plague come nigh thy dwelling. For he shall give his angels charge over thee, to keep thee in all thy ways. They shall bear thee up in their hands, lest thou dash thy foot against a stone." (Psalm 91:2, 9–12.)

So, dear friend, be not afraid. You, too, can have angels to bear you up. Meanwhile, bring some joy to yourself. Do you recall these beloved lines from Saadi?

> If of thy mortal goods thou art bereft,
> And from thy slender store two loaves alone
>   to thee are left,
> Sell one, and with the dole
> Buy hyacinths to feed thy soul.

Now, that is what I call being unafraid and facing trouble with panache!

2

I Cry
for You

cry for you," sympathized the visitor at my hospital door. She stretched a bounteous bouquet ahead of her as she walked closer to my bed. "Here are winter flowers on this snowy day. They are to shine away sadness and let you know that I care."

They were perky straw flowers, each vibrant color bunched to itself and the whole palette tied together with thin satin streamers gracefully knotted, bowed, and rippling from stiff stems. It was an unusual and lovely offering. More than that though, the bouquet hid her withered arms, deformed since birth.

And she cried for me!

Among the rude hospital interruptions, among the painful humiliation of a hospital stay, here came a healing message: color against dark discouragement; dried blooms to last beyond a time of trial; a mere acquaintance, who knew affliction, to turn my heart around.

Whatever we have to weep over, there are others always with greater grief. It is after all not only what we do about what happens to us, but how we feel about affliction as a principle of life.

"Smell the perfume of flowers," said Helen Keller, a prime example of victory over affliction, of contribution when there might have been only life as a lump. Fifty years ago the Utah School for the Deaf honored Miss Keller by exhibiting her full text on the matter:

"I who am blind [and deaf] give one hint to those who see. Use your eyes as if tomorrow you would be stricken blind. And the same method can be applied to the other senses. Hear the music of voices, the song of a bird, the mighty strains of an orchestra, as if you would be stricken deaf tomorrow, touch each object as if tomorrow your tactile sense would fail. Smell the perfume of flowers, taste the relish of each morsel, as if tomorrow you could never smell and taste again. Make the most of every sense; glory and beauty which the world in all facets of pleasure reveals to you through the several means of contact which Nature provides. But of all the senses, I am sure that sight is the most delightful."

We who are blessed with all the senses can have only scant appreciation for that message of Helen Keller. Yet it stands as important counsel for overcoming affliction of any kind.

I recall the day she spoke to war veterans in a hospital for servicemen and gave essentially the same counsel. She was touring such facilities to give courage to severely wounded young men. Morale is always the critical problem and concern in such facilities. The body will heal or not through medical help and God's miracles. But the condition of the soul, the spirit, the mind—establish that fact as you will—is the work of the individual. Helen was there to help with perspective, to motivate. This she did magnificently.

Her story is well known, but to be in her presence and feel her strength was to know the possibilities in a human soul to overcome, to become powerful in goodness and accomplishment *no matter what.* To be sick or afflicted in some way is not the issue. It is to live, to do, to become, to strive, to find ways to flourish. To enjoy peace and ease might be nice but certainly not necessary to inner well-being.

Watching sightless Helen Keller move about in compassion through Bushnell Hospital in Brigham City, Utah, was an important day for me. I was young and impressionable. She influenced my life. Listening to her speak, I cried for her. I cried because she couldn't hear the resounding applause when she finished. She could only feel the vibration of it from the floor through her feet and legs. She couldn't see the radiant faces of the wounded, pain-wracked veterans nor the presentation bouquet of long-stemmed flowers placed in her arms. But she buried her face in them and swiftly handled and *knew* the petals, the stems, the ribbons, even the supporting florist wire! She didn't miss much, it seemed to me, but I cried for her for all the years of frustration and deprivation and differences that she felt between herself and others. Yet she seemed richer, more compassionate, more marvelous than anyone in the hospital.

Perhaps this is the burden of this book, the message of life itself—that we be fully alert to whatever we are experiencing. It isn't just about learning and understanding. It is about feeling and becoming. It is about tenderizing the soul and heightening the grand adventure itself.

A national television news program showed a brief sequence featuring a young boy whose brain had been partially severed through surgery in an effort to cure dreadful and damaging seizures. The broad scar across his whole head was evident. A wheelchair cradled his young body. As the television camera moved in, he struggled mightily and succeeded in saying, "Goodbye, I . . . love . . . you!"

This viewer cried for him.

Those standing near him had eyes shining with tears. To be in the presence of such courage, such gratitude for another round of whatever life offers, obviously had melted them.

In the front of the chapel stood a beautiful seventeen-year-old girl dressed from hair to shoes in the latest young trends of the day. She was restrained in demeanor as she addressed the sympathetic congregation. We were especially attentive because we knew that in recent weeks her younger sister had succumbed, after a long battle, to a dreaded disease that afflicted their family. We knew that the father and yet another sister had been taken by the same disease in years past. Then three weeks ago the younger sister. Now this young woman was suffering the terrifying symptoms. There was no miracle for her family; why should there be for her? There was no cure, and life for her was now limited. She knew it. She spoke of it. Notwithstanding, she bore a strong testimony of the value of life and all its experiences. She expressed love for God and confidence in his will and judgment.

And the well, the near-well, and those afflicted who needed lifting and reminding wept together in the presence of one whose understanding of the purpose of life was remarkable.

I cried for her because of her example of faith and maturity, strength and seeming lack of fear. It wasn't what she wanted, but she was trying to be as accepting as possible.

Here's another example to consider:

The fifty-year-old mother spoke at her only son's funeral. He had been in ill health all of his life. The young man's symptoms had been complicated and extensive. Over the years he had somehow struggled, disciplined, and prayed himself into a state where he could fill a mission. On his return his condition worsened. His mother donated one of her kidneys in an attempt to save his life, but the transplant was rejected. Agonizing months later death came to the son.

The suffering of the son and the snuffing out of his life is one kind of tragedy. The family's grief at their loss was overwhelming. The demands upon a care-giving family cannot be measured. Hospital and medical bills mounted in staggering rapidity. Thinking upon the long, twenty years of suffering, I cried for this mother. Yet there she stood at the funeral, smiling through tears, to give thanks, to witness that there was joy in knowing God—one comes close to heaven with problems like these. This family knew unequivocally that God cared about them. The struggle of life was purposeful and therefore valuable.

Some lines from great thinkers and writers give perspective on this subject.

It was Charles Dickens who wrote, "And can it be that in a world so full and busy, the loss of one weak creature makes a void in any heart so wide and deep that nothing but the width of vast eternity can fill it up?" (Dombey and Son.)

Edna St. Vincent Millay wrote this interesting view on death:

> Listen, children:
> Your father is dead.
> From his old coats
> I'll make you little jackets;
> I'll make you little trousers
> From his old pants.
> There'll be in his pockets

Things he used to put there,
Keys and pennies
Covered with tobacco;
Dan shall have the pennies
To save in his bank;
Anne shall have the keys
To make a pretty noise with.
Life must go on,
And the dead be forgotten;
Life must go on,
Though good men die;
Anne, eat your breakfast;
Dan, take your medicine;
Life must go on,
I forget just why.

Emily Dickinson wrote:

After great pain, a formal feeling comes—
The Nerves sit ceremonious, like Tombs—
The stiff Heart questions was it He that bore,
And Yesterday, or Centuries before?
The Feet, mechanical, go round—
Of Ground, or Air, or Ought—
A Wooden way
Regardless grown,
A Quartz contentment, like a stone—
This is the Hour of Lead—
Remembered, if outlived,
As Freezing persons, recollect the Snow—
First—Chill—then Stupor—then the letting go—

"It is the image in the mind," wrote Colette in *My Mother's House*, "that links us to our lost treasures, but it is the loss that shapes the image, gathers the flowers, weaves the garland.''

Though a certain peace comes when suffering is ended, the death of one beloved must be reckoned with in stages. A funeral, the closing of the grave, the end of the day do not bring relief from loss. It takes remembering and new positioning in the heart and mind of the bereaved.

When sorrow in its acute form finally passes, there comes a kind of silence that is different from the numbing stillness of early mourning. At each such stage I cry for you. I know this hurt. Only reunion assuages this weeping eye and heart. And the wait seems long. A kind of home-sickness wells up now and then that "others" don't recognize or understand. They assume you have "gotten over it" or "forgotten" or made proper "substitutions."

Let's look to another kind of affliction that puts demands on us. It was a thundering blow to my husband and me to realize that being in a wheelchair makes a difference in how some people view you as a person. Following his stroke, we made our first social foray into public. People were kind to help, but some treated him like a child—as if being in a wheelchair had made him mentally invalid. They didn't know how to relate to him. I cried for him. I wish they had cried, at least for a moment, even if they couldn't think of anything to say.

I was explaining this to a young man, who was a stranger, riding beside me on public transportation. "O how I know what you mean! Look at me," he said, uncovering his humped back that had been hidden by a warm coat. "For twenty years I've been stared at; I've had to beg to get work. I am a professional chef, and people assume that I can't think or cook because of this terrible birth defect. I've had to build inner strength and thick skin to move forth in society, I can tell you. Crying doesn't help."

But sometimes we do cry. Sometimes we complain.

Sometimes we withdraw in loneliness. Sometimes we have to accept things we do not understand.

Jesus took the cross alone when the cup didn't pass. People didn't know what to do about that but weep, either. There is a lesson, too, to be learned from Joseph Smith at Liberty Jail. Remember, when you visit that shrine, that he was suffering a greater pang than personal discomfort. He was suffering also for his people, for the Saints, who had received much harsh treatment from their enemies, having had to trek 150 miles to the Missouri border in winter after being forced from their homes. He knew God's power, and he pleaded for it to be exerted to avenge the wrongs and assist the sufferers. He cried: "O God, where art thou? And where is the pavilion that covereth thy hiding place?" (D&C 121:1.) Joseph knew that God had appointed him to do a certain work. He had seen him; talked with him; been trained by him and his angels. He knew God could bring release from such humiliation, deprivation, delay from mission fulfillment. Surely it was a terrible agony to be denied relief. What was God's answer? "These things shall give thee experience" (D&C 122:7).

What was true for Joseph is true for us. On one occasion I sat in a doctor's office and watched a lovely receptionist deal with the press and problems of a busy cardiologist's patients. Skilled and courteous, she moved things along in spite of the doctor's delays. When it was my turn to go into the inner sanctum of examining rooms, I was shocked to see how disrespectfully the doctor treated her. While I was audience, this attractive woman was unfairly criticized, reprimanded, and rudely reminded of certain simple procedures. It was humiliating and hurtful for the receptionist. I could have cried for her.

Later I made it a point to talk with her about how she endured working under such circumstances. Being a new widow, she had moved to this city for a new life. Jobs were hard to come by, and she acutely needed this one. She had no choice but to take whatever constant unpleasantness the doctor felt driven to deal her, as if some scapegoat were needed. But for her it was a time of valuable experience. Interpersonal relationships are the basis of life. She had learned a new skill.

To those among us who are afflicted, crying isn't all that suffering is about. Nor does suffering mean that God has stopped loving us.

Attending to our senses, as Helen Keller suggested, we can realize that they are our avenue to God-likeness. If we can see, hear, taste, smell, touch, and feel with inner sensitivity the experiences of life, surely our sympathies for the plight of others will increase. Surely our skill in serving them will improve. Surely when they cry, we will taste salt. And as we turn to others, we are healed from the worst pain of our own hurt.

Let's Talk It Over

he tulips squeezed into the little fellow's fist were dropping, and the stems where they had been twisted free from the mother plant were already beginning to string and curl, like dandelion stems we children used to deliberately suck in and blow out on to reshape.

"Mama, you've got trouble!" he said thrusting the flowers toward her.

It was an appealing sight to this woman so grateful for motherhood, to see her bright little four-year-old and his constant companion of the same age, the neighborhood shepherdess from down the block, standing before her with their spring loot.

"Trouble? Not me," she answered. "I am one happy woman just having you here!" She snuggled the two children to her.

"Hey, Mom, the flowers—you'll mess them up. They're for you." The boy wiggled free and thrust the flowers toward her again. "Well, anyway, Mrs. Bertagnole says for me to tell you that you are in trouble."

"I am in trouble?" The unfamiliar tulips took on new meaning.

"Yes, because I picked all of these flowers. That's what she said. But I did it for you because you said you wanted some tulips, and we don't have any, and Mrs. Bertagnole had these white ones." He breathed a deep sigh and laid the tulips in his mother's lap.

She did have trouble. Why hadn't he gone next door to Troxlers' and picked tulips? the mother wondered. It wouldn't have mattered so much. They had half an acre of bright yellow and multi-striped tulips that had been in the ground many years. But Mrs. Bertagnole really didn't grow flowers. Or children!

"Darling, these are beautiful tulips. But most of all I love you for thinking of me and for coming directly home with them. Thank you!" And she hugged him again and put her face in the graceful arch of the petals. "I love you for bringing me these beautiful tulips. Now about that trouble we seem to be in. Let's talk it over. First, you forgot to get permission from Mrs. Bertagnole to pick her tulips. Second, why don't we go together to see how we can make her feel better?"

"Mom, I'm glad you are my friend."

Walter Savage Landor wrote, "When the heart overflows with gratitude, or with any other sweet and sacred sentiment, what is the word to which it would give utterance? A friend."

When heartbreak happens, when the intricacies of trouble weigh upon you, when grief has to have its day or year, someone to talk things over with is a blessing. If that person will listen, well so much the better blessing for you.

If you are among the sick and afflicted, the following suggestions might be helpful.

1. *Talk it over*

Talk it over, this consuming, wretched problem of yours, but think twice before you reveal your soul to just anybody. This is good counsel because the listener may not hold your confession sacred, or you may find yourself in a one-upsmanship game of who can tell the worst horror stories, who has the biggest load, who hurts the most. Sensitivity is needed because no doubt your friend, too, has trouble.

For example, serious and unpleasant personal illness had changed my whole life, my productivity, and peace. Once I wanted . . . no, I felt I needed . . . to talk it over, to share it with someone. An opportunity presented itself. At a social gathering several men and women stood talking, and someone made the mistake of asking me how I was feeling. I decided to tell them because I felt maybe people really did care and I had a captive audience. I launched in with both eyes flashing and my heart beating with relief. However, seconds later I shifted gears and changed the subject. Because as I looked into the eyes of the group with whom I stood, I realized I couldn't dump my troubles on any one of them. Great balls of fire, they had troubles enough of their own. Lucy's son was caught in the drug scene, and they were sorely tried physically, financially, and spiritually. He'd even tried to harm her on one sad occasion. Cameron had hip problems—two replacements, complications, overweight adding to his woes. Now his knees and back were giving out. And he was in the construction business where walking about the sites was his livelihood.

Helen was caring for her father-in-law in her home. Her husband had been killed in a car accident the year before, and yet the family still left the old man with her. For her to take care of the father-in-law's bodily needs and cope with his mental confusion and irritating ways was a more terrible trial to her than the death of her husband. Julie recently had lost her only daughter, and the grandchildren she adored were being moved by their father to another state where he and his new wife were to start a new life.

Doug was bankrupt. His reputation was in question, too. He'd been released as a bishop, and there were some financial shadows. The family was moving from their home, and the children were being difficult and rebellious. His life, his investment of self, as well as money, over the long years were down the drain. Evelyn was just out of pain clinic treatments for migraine headaches. Bob had married someone not of his religion on the promise that his wife would join and they could then worship as a family. But not only had she dropped this plan, she badgered him about taking the children, she taunted him about his church-imposed personal disciplines, and she fought paying tithing with open scorn. Hal had been excommunicated and was fighting his way through shame and healing.

So it went around the circle. And I was going to tell *my* little troubles to a group like that—or to any one of the group? No way. Then what? Keep it to myself? Pretend it didn't exist? Who could I talk it over with? I could talk it over with the Lord.

2. Talk it over with the Lord

Prayer is therapeutic. Read about Enos and his mighty struggle in prayer for a remission of his sins. He prayed all night and day. Surely our own problems demand more than a perfunctory recitation of need—or even of gratitude —as we kneel before Heavenly Father at bedtime, for example. Remember, pray that you faint not and remain steadfast in your mind in the spirit of prayer, constantly, as we are told in the Doctrine and Covenants. (See 75:11;

84:61.) In Acts 17 we are reminded that He is never far from us. "For in him we live, and move, and have our being; . . . For we are also his offspring."

3. *Set the stage for help*

In the hours of trouble and misery, as well as in times of festivity and joviality, we seek for someone with whom we can communicate our feelings. When we are sick or afflicted, sometimes all it takes to rescue us from depression, to lend strength for another go at life is a good listening ear and a guarded heart. Maybe we need to set the stage for such a blessing by making a date for "there-is-no-free-lunch" with a trusted, sympathetic friend. Maybe it will be an appointment with a dear, overworked bishop. Perhaps the answer is to unburden before a kind stranger on an airplane, someone you won't have to see again!

In Fillmore, Utah, near the center of the town there is a fast food place that features home cooking. For many years Helen Winget has not only served up the best hamburgers and shakes between Salt Lake City and St. George, Utah, but she has been a friend to many in need. The kind word, the listening ear, the generous deed, the quick answer to a traveler's questions, a bright smile, and a gentle word—all have been on her menu as she greeted the public. In recent years, this attractive woman moved a mobile home next to the little cafe. There her father-in-law and her husband, both in very poor physical condition, would rest where she could keep close watch on them and still earn their livelihood serving the public.

The amazing strength, personal discipline, and faith of this woman carried over as she dealt with others. Only a few suspected the load she carried. They noted only her compassion.

Not long ago we stopped for refreshment at Wingets'. We learned of the passing of both men from a waitress.

Then the young woman said, "O Sister Cannon, let me get Mrs. Winget. She'll want to see you."

In a few moments Mrs. Winget appeared, seeming to be vastly different. She was desperately unhappy, lonely, and feeling unneeded now that her charges were deceased. Change brings its own assault on our emotions and stability. It was a different kind of affliction she was suffering these days.

Mrs. Winget and I embraced a moment and then she said, "I needed someone's arms around me. I need someone to care about me today—someone who can understand from experience what I have been through. God brought you here today!"

It was her birthday, I learned from the waitress. We surprised her by leading the patrons of the hamburger stand in a rousing rendition of "Happy Birthday," complete with a lighted match stuck into a fudge sundae, and a small speech in tribute to a great lady because of years of friendly helping.

4. *Take time to give friendly help*

An eighty-three-year-old former bishop was interviewed shortly before he died. He was asked to identify the biggest change in the world that he had noticed over his lifetime. The thoughtful older gentleman said it wasn't technology, not man's reaching the moon, but the biggest change to affect mankind in important ways was the fact that people don't have time for each other any more.

At a certain evangelical church in downtown New York the minister insists that a person who "comes unto Christ" should back up his or her conversion with practical action.

"Christ served people," said a minister in a special television documentary on man's treatment of man in the name of God. "As soon as someone accepts Christ, we commit them to living as Christ did. We put them in the soup kitchen. We put them in the suicide wards and the well-clinics. It isn't what people say that counts," explained the Reverend Church, a son of former Senator Frank Church of Idaho; "it's what they are willing to do about what they believe."

5. *Be a nurturer, as well as a listener*

A brilliant professional man, handsome, accomplished, and sought after for social situations, sat with me one night at a festive event, oblivious to the gaiety of the gathering. He had undergone bypass surgery and was suffering the pangs of postoperative depression, life-style change, restricted professional activity, complexities of home responsibilities for an invalid wife, children who didn't know how to treat him with his current limitations, and friends who didn't have time to comfort or even to wait for his slower movements.

He said, "When I have been to a well and my bucket is filled, I can cope with my new situation and my life. But when it is empty, I am frightened, honestly, by my feelings of depression."

"We all need nurturing. It helps us cope better," I said. "Looking back on my own life, at every stage, I can see that I have done better at daily coping when there has been a kind of nurturing, a filling of my cup, warm fuzzies of approval. And I admit it now."

How sorely we need good, available wells—in addition to the living water God gives unto us! How helpful it is when our buckets are full of thanks to sensitive friends, wise associates, thoughtful neighbors and strangers, patient family members!

6. *What's needed most*

There is a vast amount of trouble out there. People are truly beginning to understand that everyone has *Afflicted* stamped on his or her forehead. Sooner or later, one way or another, over and again, afflictions come. What is needed most is that we become cheerleaders and boosters for each other. We need to build and define each other's strengths. We need to encourage and reassure. We need to sympathize some and say, "Tell me about it" or "I am so sorry" or "How hard this must be for you" or "How do you cope with this sort of thing."

Emily Dickinson's few lines say it well for the most idealistic among us:

> If I can stop one heart from breaking,
> I shall not live in vain;
> If I can ease one life the aching,
> Or cool one pain,
> Or help one fainting robin
> Unto his nest again,
> I shall not live in vain.

7. *What is* not *needed*

As we seek to help others, well-meaningness is not enough to bring about the healing of the pain and stress that today's afflictions impose upon people. We do not need judgmentalism, nor uncertain trumpets touting weak principles. We do not need hindsight nor unsought counsel when at the moment all we are seeking is comfort and a certain stamina.

The key is to be helpful and not stifle the suffering victim's emotion with unsought advice or inappropriate conversation, out of keeping with the mood. That is if you choose to be one who will "stop one heart from breaking" as Emily Dickinson wrote.

For example, when my husband was in the hospital following bypass surgery, two gentlemen who meant well came to see him. It was indeed kind of them to adjust their busy schedules to check in on their friend in need. However, the visit was detrimental because they didn't seem to know how to act under sickroom circumstances. These were the elements of the situation: my husband was changed; they were inexperienced with dealing with the sick and afflicted; they were not skilled in bedside demeanor; they had never been this ill, so they didn't understand; they were not filled with Christ-like compassion. Whatever the reason, in a prolonged visit they exchanged jokes and indulged in giddy, jocular conversation. This served only to frustrate the patient and set him yet further apart as one sick and afflicted.

Meaning well isn't enough for helping and healing.

Here are two simple examples that I noted in a social gathering, and they are included here because they are practical; they show the good we can do for each other in small ways.

A candidate for public office had lost in a recent election. I watched his face grow longer, his attitude darker as several people consoled him, "Sorry you lost." And the disappointment in his own heart was magnified until one cheery lady took his arm and said, "I'm so happy you lost! Now you can join our retired group activities. We have missed you and we need you." How that man smiled. There was a pleasant future for him after all.

The other example concerns a woman taking medicinal steroids under doctor's orders; the side effects were damaging to her appearance and devastating to her ego. Some said pointedly, "Martha, you look beautiful." And she knew they were lying, or hoped they were because her self-image was suffering. She did not think that she looked beautiful at all with enormous swollen glands. In disappointment she wondered why people couldn't see the difference. Or maybe they didn't really care.

Then a lady who was known for her personal grooming and a penchant for plastic surgery, cosmetically speaking, came to Martha. She put both hands on Martha's shoulders in a gesture of concern and affection and said, "Martha, what has happened to you? What are you going through?"

Martha responded to this direct and caring approach and explained her problem. The lady quickly replied, "Martha, I have always considered you a real knockout. I am so sorry you have to endure this now. But it won't last. You're just the girl who can beat this rap! God bless you." And though Martha's eyes brimmed, her smile brightened.

Like the mother of the tulip-picking toddler, when we have trouble it may help to talk it over with God or a wise and sympathetic friend. Meanwhile, we can be such a friend. It is what the world needs more of.

4

Girded with Gladness

 field of wildflowers swept up the gentle slope from the highway to the green cliffs and the waterfall that fed the fjord we'd come to see. We had finished our small hike to the inlet and while waiting for others on our tour to come back to the bus, we dropped in the daisy field to rest. Norway was beautiful that June, and my companion and I were like girls again in this place so removed from our own lifestyle.

Talk came easily in such a setting.

My companion picked a daisy, twirled it in her hand a moment, and then began gently to pull free a petal at a time. It was an age-old act for hopeful girls.

"We've gone well beyond this!" my traveling friend said sadly.

"Not so," I countered. "We're sitting here doing it, aren't we? It's all in fun. What other criteria is there for asking a daisy to give you an answer?"

"None, of course, and I really didn't expect a proper answer from a daisy when I was young, either. The only difference is that now my security comes in *not* knowing what will happen next."

We laughed. Then I said, "My grandchildren's other grandmother, Rosebud Jacobsen, is particularly charming and also quite wise. She would agree with you. She once told me that at this stage life is so uncertain she doesn't even buy green bananas!"

"That's wonderful!" My friend finished the daisy game and then said, "See, I lose again!"

"Like buckets in a well that go down empty every time?" I suggested. "Why not be buckets coming up full? There is still so much left to do, to feel, to enjoy. . . ."

"Yes, and endure. . . ."

"You are right, of course," I agreed and then added, "but I try to remember what a psychiatrist told a friend of mine who has been saddled, so to speak, for four long, tough years with a husband plagued with advanced multiple sclerosis."

"What did the psychiatrist say that is relevant to us now?"

"He told her that enduring wasn't the glorious end of all. He insisted that she, too, had a right to live and that she should take time to be self-concerned—at least every eight days! If she didn't, she'd become ill, he warned her, then her husband would be without his remarkable caregiver."

"So everyone has problems. That doesn't lessen mine any. What are we supposed to do?" My friend was insistent and searching.

"Well, I think that we have a right to live—not only a right, but a responsibility to seek for quality in living whatever kinds of struggles we each have. Life only comes one to a customer, you know."

"So you have said on other occasions."

"There's something else. If we think of ourselves as victims, we become victims. We start doubting our ability to cope, to endure, to stand, to move the mountain, or put up with a crotchety person. We question our values and our familiar systems and our sacred beliefs. We are rendered ineffective by our own thoughts—like the centipede verse, you know."

"You mean *the* centipede?" Her mood brightened, and she recited the familiar lines:

> The centipede was happy quite
> Until the frog for fun
> Said, "Pray which leg comes after which?"
> Which wrought his mind to such a pitch
> He lay distracted in the ditch
> Considering how to run.

"Yes, that's it! Well, what we need is continuing faith —not just placid, testimony-meeting faith, but active, mood-lifting, behavior-affecting, attitude-modifying faith."

"How true that is. But how do we get that kind of faith so that it is there to sustain us when we need it? I spend a lot more time preparing lectures and tests for my English classes than I do trying to increase my faith," explained my companion.

"God isn't as concerned with time as we are. I have noticed that unlike preparations for worldly tasks, the smallest effort on our part to draw close to God and to increase in understanding of his will and his ways is rewarded immeasurably by him. We are flooded!"

"You are talking quality time, I suppose," she mused.

"Yes. I believe that before faith in self comes faith in God, which brings the kind of confidence that solving today's problems requires. I also know that I need scripture study and prayers and a valiant spirit more now than I did when I was a high school girl playing the daisy game. Don't you? There is so much at stake. There are so many and so much depending upon each of us."

"Maybe scripture study, meditation, and talking things over with a good friend like you is part of it."

"Okay, I'll buy that. I also believe that we need to feel 'girded with gladness' like that quote in Psalm 30."

"Yes, but when you've gone through what I've been through it is hard to feel glad—ever."

"You are going to be fine. You are going to make it one more round. You are not going to cave in over this particular struggle, this time of suffering. Not you, not with all you have learned in life. And what's more there will be gladness in you again. Surely you are feeling it a bit today, here and now."

She smiled and, "girded with gladness," we hooked arms while we walked back to the bus. Hanging on to someone else for a time helps in many a situation.

These lines from Psalm 30 are great and comforting: "O Lord my God, I cried unto thee, and thou hast healed me. O Lord, thou hast brought up my soul from the grave: thou hast kept me alive, that I should not go down to the pit. . . . weeping may endure for a night, but joy cometh in the morning. . . . Thou hast turned for me my mourning into dancing: thou hast put off my sackcloth, and girded me with gladness."

Probably what you need right now is emotional survival. Stability comes with learning to cope with problems until you feel "girded with gladness" in spite of what life entails. Counting on God is a basic secret to emotional stability.

For example, there comes a time when your heart is broken, your spirit is sagging, your feeling of self-worth is thin. You admit that there is reason enough for such depression in this current set of circumstances. You deserve to be somewhat unstrung, even devastated. But you learned long ago that fruitless crying delays resolution to problems, and life is about problems. Therefore, it is good you've learned how to work through them, isn't it? So score one for you!

You check out your emotional symptoms to discover why you are weeping instead of being someone who stifles grief or hurt by dutifully doing one's duty no matter what milk is spilled. Whatever the details behind this particular trauma, the fact is that you are feeling blue because you are dwelling on the dark night with its disappointments. Instead, look to morning when joy cometh, thanks be to God who made the sun to rise as well as to set.

When you turn to the Lord in need and in increasing faith, the comfort always comes. It has never proven otherwise. That is the thing to remember. And when he has helped you, you quickly turn to help others.

A lovely lady named Linda came by to see me one frazzled, dumpy day. She had a pumpkin pie in hand.

"What have I done to deserve this?" I happily asked.

"I don't know, really. I needed to do a good deed, to live outside myself in love. Your name came to mind. Maybe I was inspired—who knows? Anyway, don't thank me, thank the Lord. But if the pie isn't good you can blame me!"

"What do you mean, you *needed* to do a good deed?"

"I woke up burdened with my grief. I'm just not used to being a widow yet, I guess, and I turned to the Lord, of course. You'd think he'd get so sick of me. Well, a few precious minutes of communion with God and I realized that though my husband wasn't resurrected at that moment, I wasn't alone. I had a few debts to pay, that's all, and so I needed to do a good deed.''

And you know, that can be true with any of us. Maybe we need to do more good deeds to find ourselves ''girded with gladness.''

Of course, we weep. Of course we cry out over a lost loved one, a misplaced envelope of money desperately needed, a broken heirloom, a negative diagnosis from the doctor, a disappointment in a child, a hurt from a friend, a wrecked car—whatever! But we allow the weeping to be only for the night. We are in control. Our hand is in God's. We know that joy will come in the morning—we're not exactly sure *when* morning will come, but come it will, trailing clouds of joy!

Did you know that the scriptures tell us we should weep for the loss of a loved one? ''Thou shalt live together in love, insomuch that thou shalt weep for the loss of them that die. . . . And it shall come to pass that those that die in me shall not taste of death, for it shall be sweet unto them.'' (D&C 42:45–46.)

I like that.

Here is something Frederic Lawrence Knowles wrote a hundred years ago:

> Joy is a partnership.
> Grief weeps alone.
> Many guests had Cana.
> Gethsemane had one.

Mostly we endure what we must endure on our own. Whether we turn to God, his wisdom and will, and whether we seek the comfort of a friend is up to us. Because of God we all are "girded with gladness." And this goes a long way to help us to endure gracefully those vicissitudes that inevitably come in life.

Does God bless the sick and the afflicted? He does. He will. Sometimes through a heavenly outpouring and sometimes through a friend at hand. But one thing this world needs, according to President Gordon B. Hinckley, is a generation of men and women of learning and influence who can and will stand up and in sincerity, and without equivocation, share their knowledge that God lives and that Jesus is the Christ. It is well also, in the midst of affliction, to consider how bounteously our table is spread and to let others know that we know this.

I have a little rumpled piece of paper containing a message-for-me that was typed on it one day long past when I determined not to be crushed by the present nor fearful of the future. These are those words:

If it must be so, let's not weep or complain
If I have failed, or you, or life turned sullen.
We have had these things; they do not come
 again,
But the flag still flies and the city has not fallen.

This expresses the real reason the flag flies in front of our house. We love America, yes, but flying a flag is our way of saying, "We're okay in here. The city hasn't fallen! The world isn't at an end! What is even more, there are daisies aplenty coming up each spring with petals that can be pulled to make a game of life or to add beauty to the day. Today's problems no doubt will be replaced by tomorrow's, but there is joy in our mornings and we are 'girded with gladness' because of God's goodness."

5

The Moveable
Feasts

ice deeds to the suffering in the form of flowers and food carried from one house to another is a healing custom in our culture.

Being sick and afflicted when you are the mother in the home can be absolutely terrifying. Why, something serious could happen, and the ladies on the block could show up to help before your loved ones could hose the place out!

Phyllis Diller once told how she handled this situation. When visitors came to her door when she least expected them, and her house was a sight even for squinty eyes, she was prepared. She would display on the mantel a couple of old "get well" cards she'd saved for such moments. Then she'd put on a long face and sag to the door.

To the cards on the mantel add a supermarket vase with plastic flowers, and you'll get more sympathy. Neighbors may bring in a moveable feast, and that will take care of dinner!

When we were busy mothers, a dear friend and I used to have a pact that if one of us died the other would rush over ahead of the Relief Society sisters and straighten up the house to forestall any gossip. Meanwhile, in those days I had two rules to live by in time of crisis and affliction: 1. Keep your underwear drawer in order. 2. Return every casserole dish promptly to its owner.

In a class I was taking, a seminary teacher once explained that some women operated under the misconception that all they had to do to make it to the celestial kingdom was to pray, read a little scripture, and deliver their "sacred casseroles to the sick and afflicted." He suggested that perhaps we women make too much of our food offerings, but we knew he'd never had to feed a family two days after a new baby was born or surgery performed, or he'd never have talked that way.

Sacred casseroles? They are absolutely lifesavers most of the time.

Years ago when a new baby had swelled our family ranks, we accepted the kind offer of a casserole from a woman at church whom we really didn't know.

On the appointed day she came to our door at dinnertime, casserole in hand. We were grateful but also surprised because she came in with the steaming dish and said, "Well, isn't the table set? I have a meeting at seven, and I thought maybe we could eat first."

We could eat first?

We had four children under five, and our kitchen area looked as if it would self-destruct momentarily. Actually I believe I looked the same way and frankly would have preferred it to rousing my energy level and downing my ego to the point where I could entertain this beautifully groomed lady, this childless wonder.

In my weakened condition, I not only had to get the table set, the children subdued and cleaned, myself restored, but I had to come up with something to eat along with the casserole!

Meanwhile the lady sat down and visited with my husband.

But I have to hand it to her, she did stick it through one of our family meals. When she left she took the remaining casserole with her. "I can use it for lunch tomorrow," she explained unabashedly.

This is one of our family's favorite stories that begins with "will you ever forget the time that Sister So-and-So came to dinner?"

But the casserole was terrific, and we've used the recipe for many years.

Sister So-and-So's Tamale Pie

1 cup cornmeal
1 tsp butter
1½ cups milk or
1 can cream of
   mushroom soup
1 onion diced
½ tsp chili powder
1 medium can
   tomato sauce

1 cup cooked corn
1 lb ground beef
salt, pepper, Italian
   seasoning to taste
1 cup grated cheddar
   cheese
1 can large olives
   (optional)

Saute onion and ground beef. Cook until meat is no longer pink. Add the rest of the ingredients, mixing well. Pour into buttered casserole. Bake ½ hour to 45 minutes at 350°. Sprinkle grated cheese on top and garnish with olives, if desired. Bake ten minutes more.

Here's a different slant on taking food to the neighbors.

The daffodils Nedra Warner had poked into a bean pot were for the centerpiece of a moveable feast that our son and his sons were to enjoy. His wife had just passed away, leaving three little boys below kindergarten age with their dad. Nedra had come to help the afflicted.

"Life can't be a picnic every day," she announced when the door opened and the four faced her, their frozen hearts matching the snowy day behind her. "But today you are going to have one!"

The mood changed when this rare and lovely neighbor swept in with a picnic basket crammed with all manner of delightful picnic fixings. And the daffodils. The children quickly caught the spirit and helped spread the checked cloth in the center of the living room floor. As a center-piece toddler Jared plunked himself down with the pot of daffodils, and the party was on.

What a departure—a picnic in the living room with Dad nodding approval! Nedra hadn't brought a casserole —not for a parlor picnic. She'd packed food fit for fussy children.

Cookie cutters had turned sandwiches into intriguing shapes—animals, angels, and stars. The names of the children were printed with cheese squeezed from a tube on the top of each sandwich. The carrot and celery strips were skinny slivers that a child could chew. Everything was prepared with the little ones in mind. Wisely, she let them discover the treats without the bustling about of the typical do-gooder. Nedra brought her moveable feast, her condolences, and left the bereaved family to enjoy their feast in privacy, all happier for her efforts.

Nedra is a real flower lady. She never forgets flowers for each guest at the birthday lunches, the Christmas breakfasts, the grand occasions and the tender moments, and the simple gatherings of two people who haven't seen each other for a time. She brings a single bloom or a stem of fragrant herbs when a friend is counted among the sick and afflicted or is suffering some inner struggle. The flowers often are from her own garden, or they may be a florist's custom creation reflecting her careful taste, but they are there as a sign of life and hope.

This reveals incredible caring for others. For it is a nuisance, really, isn't it? The thought must crowd its way into the flood of things a busy mother has on her mind. The flowers must be gathered or gone for. Then they must be remembered before one is out the door and in the car! They have to be carried in with all else a woman always has in her hands when she leaves home. But with a single-mindedness, with only the thought of lifting others, somehow in a variety of settings, Nedra manages the miracles as she unobtrusively slips her flowers or her casseroles into "healing position."

Once when a truly tough and traumatic change had been imposed upon my life, the whole experience was softened for me, every day for a whole year, by the arrival at the beginning of each work week of a rose in a vase. It was sent anonymously, delivered by a stranger, and the florist would not reveal the donor. It was a happy surprise that grew with the weeks. It was exciting. It was comforting. Nedra's thoughtfulness came through one more time.

On an assignment in Idaho I was met at the airport by Donna Thompson, who was my official hostess for the event. As we drove to her home, it was the dinner hour and there were certain "dear shut-ins' " who were counting on Sister Thompson's bringing them a "bite to eat."

I sat in the car as she delivered her moveable feasts of baked beans and chocolate sheet cake. I watched from the car with interest as Donna trudged up some steep steps, balancing the food. Apparently the old woman who responded to Donna's knock had been sitting just inside, counting the minutes until she came because the door opened at once. She lifted her arms up in front of her in mock surprise, then threw them around Donna's neck, nearly unbalancing the sheet cake. Then she kissed her on each cheek and cried, "You angel! You angel of mercy! You didn't forget me."

Anyone who knows Donna Thompson knows full well that she is an angel of mercy, but she also is a very good cook. Here is her superb chocolate sheet cake recipe which cuts nicely into several small cakes just the right size for the sick and afflicted.

Donna's Chocolate Sheet Cake

2 cubes butter	½ tsp salt
1 cup water	1 tsp baking soda
2 Tbsp cocoa	4 eggs
2 cups flour	1 tsp vanilla
2 cups sugar	1/4 cup milk

Bring butter, water, and cocoa to a boil. Meanwhile sift together flour, sugar, salt, and baking soda. Pour hot mixture over flour mixture. Add eggs, vanilla, and milk. Mix well. Pour into greased, floured sheet or jelly roll pan. Bake twenty minutes at 350°.

Start the icing the last five minutes of baking time because the cake is frosted just as it comes from the oven.

Icing

1 cube butter	1 box powdered sugar
6 Tbsp milk	1 tsp vanilla
3 Tbsp cocoa	½–1 cup chopped nuts

Heat together butter, milk, and cocoa. Do not boil. Sift in powdered sugar. Stir in vanilla and nuts. Frost as soon as the cake is done.

For a time after I'd had surgery on both feet, I was a real Hobble Hattie. When the phone rang one morning before breakfast and I learned that there was an offering by the front door, my heart sang. Any help was welcome and appreciated . . . especially a pie.

The caller said she'd left a fresh peach pie while doing her pre-dawn jogging. She called to be sure we'd get the pie before the sun did.

Hallelujah! Peach pie! Help for body and soul.

I opened the front door to a moveable feast. Indeed! Billions—no trillions—of tiny black ants moved en masse up to the doorway, over the threshold and all over what I supposed had been a fresh peaches and cream pie. It looked like blackened Cajun whatever.

I didn't know there were that many ants in all the world. Now I was not only among the afflicted, I was really sick!

I wept as I gathered up that crawling, creeping mess, holding it at arm's length and enduring the creatures shifting up my hands and arms, to dump it into the garbage.

When I finally got up the nerve to tell the family at dinner where their dessert was, we laughed and laughed and laughed about the march of the ants. One of my little darlings wanted to retrieve the pie for Show and Tell the next day at school. Everybody laughed some more, but the good that offering did our dispositions made up for the taste treat we had missed while the ants had their moveable feast.

The recipe is a good one, however, and you can substitute canned or home bottled peaches or apricots for fresh peaches with equal success.

Butterscotch Peach Pie

3 to 4 cups peaches
½ cup brown sugar
1 Tbsp flour
dash salt
juice from ½ lemon,
    plus zest

¼ cup juice from fruit
    (syrup or pressed)
¼ cup butter

Place peaches in pastry-lined pan. Combine sugar, flour, salt, fruit juice, and butter in sauce pan. Cook and stir until thick. Remove from heat. Add lemon juice and zest. Pour over peaches. Place crust on top and bake at 425° for 30 minutes. Optional: brush top crust with lightly beaten egg white, sprinkles of sugar, or cream.

Perhaps you were among the privileged to see the fine foreign film *Babette's Feast*. It's enough to urge you to sign up for a French cooking class—at least to spruce up your food offerings to the needy. There is a wonderful bit of subordinate business that is sort of a before-and-after-Babette incident that reveals basic truth about human nature. For years the minister's two maiden daughters had been delivering soup or gruel to shut-ins. The film shows an old man accepting their offering in gratitude. That is until Babette came along with rare cuisine. Babette's pottage was such a true delight to him that after she went away, the old man turned up his nose when the broth of the good sisters was placed before him.

How soon we are spoiled.

I recall a day when I was well after an illness, and the neighbors had ceased their moveable feast parade to our door. One of our young sons complained, "Mom, when can you get sick again?" There was great longing in his expression. No doubt you have had a similar experience in your family. Children are such wise innocents as well as impressionable.

You see, our children had developed gourmet taste buds with the likes of Martsie Lowder's Company Stew. The recipe follows:

Martsie's Company Stew

3 pounds beef chunks*	2 bay leaves
8 large carrots	1 pkg onion soup mix
cut in four pieces	1 can cream of
8 large potatoes	mushroom soup
cut in four pieces	1 can cream of celery
Optional: 2 onions	soup
cut in four pieces	

Place all ingredients in a dutch oven and, if desired, drizzle with a small can of tomato sauce. Cover with a lid that will close tightly. Bake 8 hours at 275°.
*Note: Chicken or turkey chunks may be substituted.

There is a relative on the Cannon side who, over the years, has taken a day off now and then to make numerous little meat loaves. Janath wraps them and freezes them against somebody's need. She is always prepared to do the good deed. The slightest sniffle on my part would bring a hopeful question from one child, "Mom, will we get to have meat loaf sandwiches this week?"

Children don't understand that just because Mom has a headache or something it doesn't automatically push the family to the top of some good soul's help list for the sick and afflicted!

If you are in this program of being of use to your fellow families, I do believe it is good to be prepared with make-ahead meals. I don't know about you, but my own efforts at taking a moveable feast to the needful often have ended in disaster—the cake sags or the casserole doesn't set up. It's nice to have things made ahead when the pressure isn't on.

School lunches are often a problem in a household where mother is ill. Real neighborly help is to come up with something to solve that morning bottleneck. When I was about fourteen my mother was struggling with inner ear disease. Often when she couldn't get up because of severe dizziness, Dad would roust me from the solid sleep only teenagers know and send me forth to make the school lunches. These were mornings I dreaded. The assignment itself was bad enough, but then I had to live with the complaints about those lunches from my brothers when they got home from school!

As a result, I often have taken calzone to families with school children. Calzone is seasoned meat between biscuit dough and can be used for the lunch box or a casserole meal, depending on how the cook cuts it. A moveable feast of calzone, crisp vegetables, and cookies forms the basis of an adequate lunch for Dad or the children.

Calzone

1 lb ground lean beef or turkey breast	¼ tsp Tabasco sauce
½ cup chopped onion	1 tsp salt
½ cup grated Swiss cheese	2 Tbsp chopped parsley baking powder
¾ cup grated Parmesan cheese	biscuit dough
1 large egg, beaten	1 egg, slightly beaten

Cook meat and onion over low heat until done but not brown. Stir with fork while cooking to break up meat. Remove from heat and cool. Mix in cheeses, egg, Tabasco, salt and parsley. Place 1 square of bis-

cuit dough in a 9x9x1¾ inch pan. Spread meat mixture over dough; cover with another square of dough.
Brush with slightly beaten egg yolk. Bake at 400° for
25 to 30 minutes. Cool and cut into slices. Delicious.
This recipe yields one dozen finger sandwiches which
freeze well and are ready without a fuss to be used as
a sandwich in a lunch box.

Oh, blessed is the moveable feast manager who brings
a generous offering of prepared vegetable snacks! In a
recent illness of mine, the best moveable feast that came
my way was from Ruby Haight who prepared several single
servings of steamed vegetables, ready to pop in the
microwave for a nourishing meal. Each individual serving
was magazine picture quality because the vegetables were
so attractively arranged in the baking dish. Ruby used a
garnish of red or yellow pepper strips and threads of red
Bermuda onions to center circles of zucchini, carrot,
celery, mushroom, young summer squash, and tiny new
potatoes. And then there were clusters of kidney beans,
cauliflower, and broccoli. Parmesan cheese and a dob of
nonfat yogurt gave Ruby's treats a gourmet look but they
could still pass the most stringent nutrition guidelines of
Prevention Magazine. Served with Ruby's compassionate
smile, her delicious moveable feasts brought special solace
to this sick and afflicted woman.

Some years ago in Nova Scotia I learned that the sick
and afflicted were those people who drove four hundred
miles to attend a church conference and often had no place
to stay when they arrived. The stalwart Saints in the area
would open up their homes, but there simply was no
money to buy extra food. However, these people were re-
sourceful as well as faithful. The loaves and fishes took the
form of local blueberries. The wild berries were picked in
season, and the people used assembly line production
methods to turn blueberries into quantities of pies,
muffins, cobblers, and preserves for whole wheat bread.

These frozen goodies were then brought forth on conference weekend, and the faithful thrived solely upon these refreshments.

I broke my neck there in Halifax and when I finally got home to recuperate, imagine my delight as specially packaged frozen blueberry pies were sent with the love of the people.

Such goodness!

Mary and Sid Foulger have a spacious, interesting home in the area of the nation's capital. Their generous welcoming of people has worked wonders in the lives of those who are lonely, stricken, heart-sick, confused, or teetering dead center about the meaning of life. Mary collects people like some garner flowers from a field. There are many who are struggling, and blessed are they who find their way to her door.

One beautiful evening I watched radiance return to the faces of famous and obscure people alike as they came to one of her informal open houses. There are many private places and comfortable conversational settings in the Foulger home where people can mingle, talk, and forget stress.

On this particular occasion a buffet of nourishing food put people at ease because it seemed that even the food was designed to start conversations. We were no more strangers when we tasted and talked about the huge crystal bowl filled with colorful salad of red cabbage, purple grapes, and green avocado.

If you prefer having people to your home when they are in need, rather than moving a feast to theirs, consider Mary's special slaw. She's shared the recipe.

Mary Foulger's Special Slaw

Slice red cabbage finely. Marinate in salted water for an hour or so. Drain well. Toss with purple grapes, halved and seeded. Arrange in your best bowl and garnish with avocado.

Mary Foulger's Poppy Seed Dressing

½ cup sugar	2 cups salad oil
2 tsp dry mustard	⅔ cup tarragon
2 tsp salt	vinegar
3 Tbsp fresh	2 Tbsp poppy seed
onion juice	

In a blender mix all ingredients except poppy seed. Remove from blender and stir in poppy seed. Drizzle over the slaw and chill overnight.

One thing we all can be certain of in the activity of comforting the sick and the afflicted is that any moveable feast is positively affected by the innate traits of the human race, the law of averages, and the higher incentive to please that some people have over others. I was sitting at a luncheon with a group of women, and one was telling about the kind deeds that had been performed for her by her neighbors when she was ill. She mentioned bread sticks brought in by Colleen Maxwell and added, "They were so good that they were the turning point in my recovery."

Someone else had received some of Colleen's famous bread sticks, too, and laughed, "They are so good it's almost worth becoming ill just to get some."

Colleen Maxwell's Famous Bread Sticks

1 pkg yeast	1 Tbsp honey
1½ cups warm water	1 tsp salt
1 Tbsp malted	4–5 cups
milk powder	unsifted flour

Dissolve yeast in warm water. Mix in malted milk powder, honey, and salt. Gradually mix in unsifted flour. Mix to dough consistency and allow to rise just slightly before shaping into a dozen fat sticks. Bake fifteen minutes at 400°.

We had been blessed with bread sticks from the Maxwells at the time of my father's funeral. I put them on the table with a bowl of apricot jam and started an argument.

"This apricot jam has pineapple in it," said one visitor. "That will ruin the bread sticks."

"No way can you ruin these bread sticks," I countered. "Someone brought this jam by this afternoon. Don't you like pineapple?"

"I just don't like pineapple in apricot jam. If God wanted pineapple in apricots he'd have put pineapple where the apricot pits are!"

"Oh!" I said, quick to learn, and offered her another kind of preserves. However, accepting all things—including the sacred casseroles and the pineapple-apricot jam—with thankfulness is proper demeanor for visitors as well as for the sick and afflicted, it seems to me.

I will never forget making a batch of chili for some neighbors who appeared to be in real need. Carrying the baby on one hip and the pot of chili on the other, I trudged through the snow across the street and down the block to their home. The door was opened by the lady of the house wearing a bedraggled wrapper and an old sock around her throat. She looked dreadful and in need of my heartening chili. At least that is what I thought. I explained my visit, told her what was in the pot, and wished them well as I handed it to her.

"Well," she sighed, "we don't eat chili. You might as well take it back home. Do you have anything else?"

One thing you learn is not to take anything like that personally. It could stifle your urge to do good deeds. If she'd tasted my chili, she just might have become a chili fan, though!

Speaking of not taking rebuffs personally, I love the incident involving tender-hearted, compassionate Joan Haskins. She is a truly appreciative person, and one Christmas season she stood by her window watching the efforts of the garbage collection crew laboring in a snowstorm. She determined to show her appreciation and made up a multi-batch of her delicious Christmas loaves. By next garbage collection day the loaves were Christmas wrapped and ready for delivery.

Joan decided not to make a big deal of herself in all of this by personally handing each man his cake. Instead she stacked them pyramid style on top of the garbage can lid. Then she went inside to stand by her window again and watch. Along came the truck and the crew. Without the slightest pause, a second glance, or a brief consideration, the eager worker took the garbage can lid with the loaves and slid the Christmas treats into the dumpster.

It has been truly said, "If it's stacked in, on, or near the containers on the curb, into the truck of garbage it goes."

And shocked Joan was left to recite to herself, "It's the thought that counts!"

Another thing you learn is to take your moveable feasts in containers that don't have to be returned, unless you're long on patience and pans. I once took chili to a large family in a new stainless steel stock pot scoured within an inch of its being. What finally came back was a stained and battered pan with a mismatched lid. I protested that this wasn't my pan, but they insisted. Well, maybe the children had been playing drums.

Men have their own special talent when it comes to brightening the day for those who are sick and afflicted. The late Ralph Reynolds, art director for LDS church magazines, had many talents. He and his wife, Jane, were the first I knew to introduce delicious homemade chunky salsa. It was delivered to us in an unusual glass jar with one of Ralph's original artistic labels.

Russell Orton is partial to sorbet. During a recent family illness it was a day for spirit lifting when Russell came bearing an armful of exotic cut flowers tied with ribbon streamers plus three kinds of sorbet to serve visitors who might drop by. Wonderful!

Russell's Basic Sorbet

2 tsp gelatine
½ cup cold water
1 cup sugar
1 cup water
½ cup lemon juice
⅓ cup orange juice
¼ tsp salt

2 cups fresh
   grapefruit juice or
   blended berries, apricots,
   or peaches
2 egg whites
1/8 tsp salt

Soak gelatine in ½ cup cold water. Boil sugar and 1 cup water together for ten minutes. Add the gelatine mix and stir until it is completely dissolved. Chill. Add lemon juice, orange juice, ¼ teaspoon salt and choice of fresh grapefruit juice or blended fruit. Chill. In separate bowl, beat egg whites with 1/8 teaspoon salt until very stiff. Fold in chilled fruit mixture and freeze in portable commercial freezer. If you use ice trays, stir frequently.

One last story about a moveable feast. I answered the door one day while the moving van people were emptying our home. I felt among the afflicted to be sure, and it was a happy sight to see a little fellow standing there with a new brown bag filled with two loaves of freshly baked stoneground wheat bread.

He handed me the sack, looked me up and down and

said, "My mother sent this, and she says you need it more than we do. Do you think you need this more than we do?"

I could tell he was loath to let the loaves go.

"I'm not sure who needs the bread more, but I am mighty glad to get it," I said. "I'll tell you what, come in and we'll have a feast of our own."

He came in. We sliced the warm bread and prepared it with butter and Potawattami jelly, made from the fruit of our plum trees. We had a fine talk. When he was ready to go home, I sent a jar of jelly with him. "You really need this more than I do," I explained. "Somehow a lot of the jelly from my jar ended up there on your shirt."

That moveable feast was a real success in his eyes.

I have taken my turn over the many years at delivering the moveable feast, the sacred casserole, the funeral cake, the new baby supper, the healing chicken broth, the loaf and the jug to newcomers. It is a satisfying experience to help people, however simply. It is good to give. But until one is forced to be on the receiving end, one really can't understand the value in neighborly help. I have discovered that at first being the recipient of another's goodwill is an uncomfortable position to be in. I have to admit that I resist such imposition upon my independence. But there is no better way that the great goodness of people can be appreciated. I have been overwhelmed at their willingness, generosity, their unbounded energy, their resourcefulness and tenderness, their caring and kindness.

Humbly I thank God for friends and strangers who have helped, many when there was no possible way I could return the favor. Enthusiastically I praise the children of our Heavenly Father who have heeded the teachings of the Savior and been the good Samaritans.

Moveable feasts? Food for the afflicted? Sustenance for the body is only the beginning. It's what happens to the heart and soul when somebody cares enough to thoughtfully provide picnics in winter or sorbet for visitors.

6

A Crushing
Desire to Believe

delivery man at our door held an exquisite topiary. It was a gift, and planting it for us was part of the gift. We were delighted. We decided that such a lovely rose tree should mark the entryway to our home.

It was planted next to the porch. It was pruned, mulched, fertilized, watered, and watched. At the first sign of a rosebud a lesson was learned. It was a bud of such quality and beauty that we were rewarded at once for the good care we had given our gift.

In the days to come there were other buds and blooms that flourished in spite of the high winds about our property, the dry, deep heat of the climate, and the constant battle with insects that don't "winter kill" in the desert climate. To this day it is a tree shrub of unwavering strength.

One day, Herbert Ludwig, the fine gentleman of German descent who had given us this gift, came to visit. He wanted to check on the rose tree as well as his good friends. He also wanted to talk. For him it was a down day. He was facing frightening hospital tests and was concerned about the diagnosis that would follow.

"I am not afraid of dying," said Herbert. "I am afraid of living as a stricken old man. Except for leaving my lovely wife, I would be ready to step across the bar tomorrow." He spoke of his plans and arrangements already underway "just in case." He sounded almost hopeful about such a change! Life's struggles were wearing upon him, and he temporarily lacked the strength to rise up and go through it all again.

Herbert had lived an admirable—even enviable—life with financial success, church and community contribution and recognition. He and his wife had touched many lives. But now all that lay in the past, and Herbert saw no joyful future ahead.

I reminded him of his gift to us as we walked out of our front door. We touched one of the late summer roses of peace white on the topiary and spoke of the imagery of this plant that had reached and sent forth vigorous, healthy shoots of unwavering strength. These shoots were symbolic and were more important to us at the moment than the beauty of the blossoms. We had problems of our own, you see, and welcomed reminders of the good life.

"God requires as much of us as the rose, Herbert," I suggested. "We all need to cultivate attitudes that bring forth unshakable strength and witness of faith."

"Yes, and we need to believe in God and his plan. We need to be examples. I just don't know if I am up to it."

"You are, Herbert. Your whole life proves you are."

It was a reminder to Herbert, not a teaching moment. Friends, in time of need, can do this for each other by going over familiar principles to live by, one more time.

Reflecting on our personal testimony and understanding of God can be healing for all of us. My brother called me once and expressed such a beneficial thought to me. He had been listening from another room while his wife practiced a scriptural reading with the piano accompanist.

His wife, Virginia, is a professional elocutionist, in demand for public appearances because of her great talent and good spirit. She has advanced degrees and teaching credentials in speech therapy with years of experience helping others. She also has a firm testimony that God lives. Her personal physical struggles have proven to her that God also cares. This quality adds spiritual depth to her performances. People feel this.

As my brother listened to her rehearsal, he recognized the blessing that spirituality brings to life: a testimony of God and an understanding of self-worth make a difference. Aldon reflected about people who claim no faith in God. He said to me, "If there isn't a Higher Power, a master creator, a personal God such as we hold so dear, how can one explain music and sacred words that can stir our souls? How do we explain flowers, myriads of trees, seashells, and sunsets? What of the warmth of animals and the talents of people? How do we explain the everlasting spirit of man and the vibrations between heaven and earth—between certain people with certain other people? And what of miracles? My wife is a living miracle!"

Life does have purpose beyond the obvious. Struggle, physical pain, disappointment, even despair, it seems to me, present opportunities for learning, and therefore increase our joyful responses.

These demands on our soul bring forth choice blessings that can prepare us for whatever is ahead and for all eternity. Such a grand and hopeful statement of belief!

When you are struggling, downcast, frightened, reach out beyond yourself to God. He is there. He may not, for whatever reason, at once wipe out your pain and problems. However, as you keep reaching toward him, your faith will be heightened.

Inevitably when affliction hits, doubts seem to crowd the mind. But if you desire to know, if you ache to believe, if you take that first step toward God, he will rush forth to meet you and flood you with proof.

The Lord has challenged us with these words: ". . . prove me . . . if I will not open you the windows of heaven, and pour you out a blessing, that there shall not be room enough to receive it" (Malachi 3:10).

A blessing so marvelous that there shall not be room enough to receive it? Wonderful! But the question is do you know a blessing when you get one! Or is it true that God's will is hidden by self-will? This may be the very area of faith that needs some working on, some scriptural research, from prayerful pondering, some spiritual mulching, pruning, and feeding, if you will. When the desire to believe in God, to believe that he cares about you particularly, at this moment of affliction, to believe he can bless you according to what is best for you—when that moment comes, it is a kind of "crushing desire to believe" that can bring great peace.

Admiral Byrd had a crushing desire to believe. When I was a school girl I learned this with great benefit to my life. We studied his grand adventure in the Antarctic. I was fascinated with the man. In later years I had a friend who married a man who had accompanied Byrd on several expeditions and that made the whole thing more relevant, of course.

But in those school days Admiral Byrd was our current hero who broke vast barriers of the unknown. I was given a book written by him titled *Alone*, and I have had personal pleasure over the years reading it again and again. His expressions of what he learned in those days, some of which are included in the following paragraphs, are enlightening even years later.

For example, on one expedition Byrd's personal fortitude was tested mightily. He was alone. Worse, he was weighted down with loneliness. And he had ample time to think, to question, to mentally wrestle with values and ideas he'd once held sacred but which seemed far away at such a time. He developed what he called a *"crushing desire to believe."* So Byrd sought a place apart, a formal solitude where he could reach out for understanding and strength, for the will to go on.

On that particular afternoon Byrd stood looking over the Great Barrier, feeling beauty and power in its strangeness from the rest of the world. It was incredibly still and mysterious. He thought of the orderliness in nature—the sameness in stars, sunrise, sunset, ebb and flow of the tide, and the rhythmic change of the season. To him they showed the sure hand of a master power.

Suddenly, standing there in the engulfing quiet, amid space and the harmony of uncluttered stretches of the end of the earth, Byrd felt his oneness with *the power that generates all of life.* "I am not alone," he thought. "For those who seek it, there is inexhaustible evidence of an all-pervading intelligence."

At last he went back to his shack and wrote the following lines: "The coldest cold on the face of the earth is manufactured here and I am filled with warmth . . . harmony, that was it! That was what came out of the silence—the gentle rhythm, the strain of a perfect chord, the music of the spheres, perhaps. The conviction came that that rhythm was too orderly, too harmonious, too perfect to be a product of blind chance—that therefore, there must be purpose in the whole and that man was part of that whole and not an accidental offshoot. It was a feeling that transcended reason that went to the heart of a man's despair and found it groundless!"

In our own time, I have been deeply moved by the announcement from California "stargazers" that they have witnessed the birth of an enormous new galaxy. There apparently was no surprise in this announcement. Astronomers have long suspected there were multitudes of as yet uncharted galaxies in the endless heaven. However, the assurance of continuity in the universe on a very impressive scale was now evident.

As Admiral Byrd and the California astronomers felt, so we must come to feel—that this harmony in all of the universe includes us!

That can make all the difference in how we feel about ourselves and in how we choose to respond to whatever good or ill falls our lot, as well.

A crushing desire to believe fosters prayer. Reaching out to heaven is really prayer in its most urgent form. It is an effort on our part to be worshipful, to *want* God to be there! The result of such yearning, yielding, hoping, and reaching can be measured in terms of increased well-being, greater physical buoyancy, intellectual awakening, moral vigor, and of joy itself. There also comes a keener understanding of the underlying relationship between God and man and man and man.

Alexis Carrel has been credited with these lines: "Only in prayer do we achieve that complete and harmonious assembly of body, mind, and spirit which gives the frail human its unshakable strength."

The crushing desire to believe is often first introduced by a longing to endure the day or the trial, to be brave enough to plough through the immediate problem, whether faith is perfect or not. Take life—and faith—a step at a time, may be another way of saying it.

There is a poem written by someone unknown to me that is worth reading again. It is in the form of a prayer. It is addressed, then, to God whom the author accepts. But it deals with that haunting need we have—even if we admit to God—that perhaps in us there is a weakness that makes true faith impossible. We need to believe enough to be brave!

> God, make me brave for life: oh, braver than this.
> Let me straighten after pain, as a tree straightens
>   after the rain
> Shining and lovely again.
> God, make me brave for life; much braver than
>   this.
> As the blown grass lifts, let me rise
> From sorrow with quiet eyes,
> Knowing Thy way is wise.
> God, make me brave; life brings
> Such blinding things.
> Help me to keep my sight;
> Help me to see aright
> That out of dark comes light.

Another good thing to remember is the wise counsel from old King Benjamin that is recorded in Mosiah 4:9, where we are told to believe in God; to believe that he is, and that he created all things, both in heaven and in earth. "Believe that he has all wisdom, and all power, both in heaven and in earth; believe that man doth not comprehend all the things which the Lord can comprehend." If this is true, and I believe firmly that it is, we can take comfort in the fact that with God in charge all things will at last come together for our good. Just because *we* don't understand does not mean that God doesn't. If there is any question about this in your heart or mind, perhaps you need to study again about the very nature of God and your relationship to him.

I reminded my friend of the rose tree to put his hand in God's again. To trust in God's plan—God's timetable—is an act of bravery as well as faith. This is true for you, as well. As long as you keep your mind on Jesus Christ and not on your immediate troubles, you will find you do have the strength to handle whatever comes.

Faith without works is impossible for a man like Herbert, however, and probably for someone like you. With Herbert we talked about his making a trip back to Germany in the spring for long postponed reunions. It is something to look forward to; it is an act of consuming belief.

Now, what are your plans?

7

Tune in to Christ

agnificent spring blossoms and spring fragrance marked our walk from the Plaza Hotel to the Tavern on the Green in Central Park. Our New Yorker nephew suggested this early morning walk. He wanted us to see the park at its best.

At that hour that path was the finger of God in a city of ultimate worldliness.

Later, over lunch in the Tavern, we talked of this dichotomy. Our nephew related the familiar story that indicates the challenge of being in tune with Christ in New York City, even in a park filled with God's own lovely creations.

It seems that the world-famous naturalist John Burroughs was taking a morning walk through Central Park in New York City. As usual, he was tuned in to the sounds of nature rather than the sounds of the city. Suddenly the most unusual song of a bird filled the air. Burroughs looked about for someone else who might have heard it. There were people aplenty in the park, but no one seemed to have noticed the bird's song. There was no one with whom he could share this wonder of nature!

Were the noises of city life so demanding that the song of a bird was stifled? He wondered. And then by way of experiment he took a coin from his pocket and dropped it on the concrete sidewalk. The soft clink didn't escape the joggers or strollers, the kite fliers or the ball tossers. Heads turned at the soft sound of money.

Burroughs was not only amazed but disappointed that mankind had gone so far adrift as to respond to the clink of the coin while a lovely birdcall went unnoticed.

On one of our trips to Israel there was a gentleman on the tour bus—we'll call him Bob—who came burdened with the latest equipment for recording the experience. This became a kind of nuisance to the group. We were eager pilgrims, anxious for each experience, while he was a photographer and audio recorder anxious to record everything to experience later. Consistently, Bob was maneuvering to get the best seat—and he always won. So we repeatedly had to wait for him or reposition ourselves, making other accommodations for his needs.

Yet I'll long remember the night of our tour group reunion some weeks later when we shared our pictures and memories. When the time came to play his video of the trip, there were some gentle jabs as people reminded each other of unpleasant delays. Many wondered if the product would be worth the watching. Then the video began, and people turned to each other in delight. It was like being there again. As the camera played across the old church on the Mount of Beatitudes and the gentle slopes beyond, the unique sound of birds filled our ears. There was exclamations from the group.

"Listen to the birds!"

"I didn't hear any birds that day!"

"Bob, why did you decide to dub in birds on this segment?"

"What kind of bird are we hearing?"

And so it went.

However, Bob hadn't "dubbed in the birds." On the tour the group had missed the birds altogether in the midst of new sights while the audio recorder had automatically picked them up. Sitting in a lovely living room without the distractions of travel, we heard the birds on the Mount of the Beatitudes. Thanks to Bob.

In a crowded supermarket a child calls out, "Mommy!" and the right lady turns. There are many of us mothers in the store, but only one woman responds to the child's call. She knows her little bird.

There is something recorded in the Savior's ministry on earth that over the generations has proved comforting to the sick and the afflicted, the lost and frightened, the unhappy and the sinful, the discouraged and the dependent. It is the image of Jesus as the Good Shepherd.

When you are sick and afflicted, close your eyes against miserable illness, fever, pain of heart and mind, worries that seem insurmountable. For a moment bring forth a mental picture of the Lord Jesus in flowing robes holding a lamb in his arms. Then remember what he has said about lost sheep:

"For the Son of man is come to save that which was lost. How think ye? if a man have an hundred sheep, and one of them be gone astray, doth he not leave the ninety and nine, and goeth into the mountains, and seeketh that which is gone astray?

"And if so be that he find it, verily I say unto you, he rejoiceth more of that sheep, than of the ninety and nine which went not astray." (Matthew 18:11–13.)

And more.

"He that entereth in by the door [to the sheepfold] is the shepherd of the sheep. To him the porter openeth; and the sheep hear his voice: and he calleth his own sheep by name, and leadeth them out. And when he putteth forth his own sheep, he goeth before them, and the sheep follow him: for they know his voice. And a stranger will they not follow, but will flee from him: for they know not the voice of strangers.

"Then said Jesus . . . again, Verily, verily, I say unto you, I am the door of the sheep. I am the good shepherd: the good shepherd giveth his life for the sheep. I am the good shepherd, and know my sheep, and am known of mine. As the Father knoweth me, even so know I the Father: and I lay down my life for the sheep." (John 10:2-5, 7, 11, 14-15.)

Minerva Teichert was a painter of remarkable talent, creative approach, and fulfilling application. She painted the Good Shepherd on a life-size canvas. Her trademark is a stroke of red somewhere in her paintings. In this one the red draws attention to the folds in the robes of the Good Shepherd, who is depicted as having just caught up a lost lamb in his arms. It is a heartening painting, warming and full of hope. She used this color again in a painting of the Savior healing the sick. Apparently she was inspired by the lines "And the Lord shall be red in his apparel, and his garments like him that treadeth in the wine-vat" (D&C 133:48).

Jesus said he knows his sheep, his followers. And in time of personal struggle it is lifting and helpful to remember that he knows you! And as you reach to know him, you can hear and feel his caring comfort.

How do you hear Jesus?

Do you recall the account given in 1 Kings 19:11-12 that says, "And, behold, the Lord passed by, and a great and strong wind rent the mountains, and brake in pieces the rocks before the Lord; but the Lord was not in the wind: and after the wind an earthquake; but the Lord was not in the earthquake: and after the earthquake a fire; but the Lord was not in the fire: and after the fire a still small voice.''

A suggestion to the struggler longing to hear Jesus is to come to know that he is and that he cares. You don't look for him in the big noise of the forces of nature. You listen deep within your soul for a still, small voice. Then you can know (*know!*) that he is talking to you, mindful of you, aware and concerned about your special problems and needs, as differentiated from what others are going through at the moment.

Let me share a sacred-to-me experience to underscore this idea. During a dreadful snowstorm pelting us on a mountain highway, the wonder of God's goodness to an individual in a given moment came home to my heart again.

My husband sat in the passenger seat, a victim of a paralyzing stroke, and I was driving under perilous conditions. Suddenly our car went into a spin and slid off the freeway shoulder and down a slope into a ditch. I tried to move the car but it was embedded.

I got out into the storm and surveyed our situation. Fortunately neither the car nor we were hurt. However, the deep, wet, freezing, fresh snow quickly covered me, the car, and our tracks. There was no way to get the car moved back to the freeway without a wrecker. There was no way I could help my husband up that hill into the line of traffic where we might pick up a ride. Understandably, no one stopped to offer aid in that treacherous situation. The snowplow hadn't widened or scraped the roads yet. The time stretched long, and the storm assaulted the scene. I was beginning to feel desperate. Then a thought occurred to me.

We were in the deep ditch—but not out of touch.

We had prayed for protection formally, as is our custom, before starting the trip that day. We prayed again as we sat buried in our car. And at last, one more time, I got out of the car to tie a red bandana on the antenna and alert the cars going by, trusting that someone would report our plight to the highway patrol. It seemed almost hopeless though, and I was frightened and frustrated. We had prayed! My husband was quite helpless in this setting. I was a mere woman! He had a relative who, some years ago, had frozen to death when their car stalled in a mountain pass while his wife went for help. This thought plagued my mind, and all calmness left me. I started to kick at the thick, encrusted ice over the headlights and radiator grill. I was angry. Then suddenly I cried out loud. Oh, I was contrite, now, and desperate. I was brokenhearted and helpless in a way only God could ease, under the circumstances. My anguish and full faith in God pushed through the falling snow, "Please dear Father in Heaven, do not let this good man's life end like this. Please, don't let him freeze to death here and now."

Naturally, I was sobbing. I turned to walk back toward the driver's seat and the miracle we needed happened, that fast. The Good Shepherd had heard my voice! A huge four-wheel drive truck had stopped. The driver and I struggled to get my six-foot-six husband out of our car and up the treacherous snowbank. It was an impossible situation.

And then in an amazing act of bravery (under the circumstances) as well as goodness, the driver of a passenger car risked stopping to pull up behind the truck. A big, strong stranger came forth and bodily got my husband up the slope and into the truck cab, disappearing as quickly as he had come. The truck driver proved to be a fine former bishop who took us the remaining two hours right to our home door.

How does a person ever repay such kindness? We are, as King Benjamin said, forever in debt to God. And to man as well. This was a frightening experience for us, but because of God's blessings it turned out well, and we learned all over again the goodness of people as well as the goodness of God.

The Doctrine and Covenants section 101:16 includes some counsel to remember: "Let your hearts be comforted," the Lord said, "for all flesh is in mine hands [*That means; everybody, including you, is known to him and in his care and keeping!*] be still and know that I am God."

At the time of the crucifixion of Christ, people in ancient America were gathered about the portion of their city, Bountiful, which remained standing after the three days of destruction and upheaval on earth. Naturally they were marvelling and conversing about all these events. "And it came to pass that while they were thus conversing one with another, they heard a voice as if it came out of heaven; and they cast their eyes round about, for they understood not the voice which they heard; and it was not a harsh voice, neither was it a loud voice; nevertheless, and notwithstanding it being a small voice it did pierce them that did hear to the center, insomuch that there was no part of their frame that it did not cause to quake; yea, it did pierce them to the very soul, and did cause their hearts to burn.

"And . . . again . . . they did hear the voice, and did open their ears to hear it; and their eyes were towards the sound thereof; and they did look steadfastly toward heaven, from whence the sound came. And behold, the third time they did understand the voice which they heard; and it said unto them: Behold my Beloved Son, in whom I am well pleased, in whom I have glorified my name—hear ye him."

Now as the people understood what was being said to them they cast their eyes up toward heaven again, and, wonder of wonders, "they saw a Man descending out of heaven; and he was clothed in a white robe, and he came down and stood in the midst of them." Then he stretched forth his hand and spoke to them: "Behold I am Jesus Christ, whom the prophets testified shall come into the world."

The people now were tuned in to him, and when Jesus had spoken these words, the whole multitude fell to the earth.

This account is described in beautiful detail in the Book of Mormon, 3 Nephi 11. But for further light and knowledge about that all-important still, small voice, you may want to begin your reading at 3 Nephi 9.

Remember, the Lord has said *who* he is, that he *is*, and the he *knows* his sheep. He has said that his sheep know him. My concern is that we sheep who are suffering and struggling, sick or otherwise afflicted, may have spent more time getting into discomforting situations than learning of him so that we will know him and recognize his voice, and therefore can follow after him.

If you are in need, tune in to Christ. Listen for the still, small, mild voice that will pierce the core of your being. It can bring you direction, comfort, peace, miracles. Read again the lines from Doctrine and Covenants 136:29; "If thou art sorrowful, call on the Lord thy God with supplication, that your souls may be joyful."

The Lord, our Good Shepherd, does not forget his promises. We should not forget his counsel.

John Burroughs's experiment with the song of the bird and the clink of a coin in Central Park was revealing, wasn't it? How much more critical it is for us to be tuned in to the Lord as the Lord is tuned in to us, waiting to be gracious to us!

8

The Word of God

he grass withereth, the flower fadeth: but the word of our God shall stand for ever." That scripture is found in Isaiah 40:8. There are those who are skilled in knowing the scriptures. They can recite one at the drop of an opportunity. They locate the proper reference in seconds. They use it with logic and facility. They may even be wise in the application of the word of God to the exigencies of life.

Most of us, however, need help in finding specific answers in the scriptures to specific problems at any given time of affliction in life. We'd be glad to obey God's commandments and heed his word when we stand at a crossroad, if we could only recall what the Lord has said in such matters. At the moment, though, we are interested solely in God's mercy and love to help us in time of suffering and anguish, struggle and affliction.

The word of God is filled with the simple, familiar things of the world and of our lives. All the easier comes the learning! All the swifter comes the comfort!

For example, the following scriptures are included that they may be readily available to you as you wrestle with being sick and afflicted. Tomorrow may, in fact, be a better day, but first let's deal with dreadful, depressing, debilitating, devastating, discouraging, disagreeable, disheartening today. This we do by turning to the word of God and reading and rereading such truth until it becomes a guiding light that is comfortable and moving to us.

"Lift up thy voice with strength; lift it up, be not afraid; say unto the cities . . . Behold your God! . . . He shall feed his flock like a shepherd: he shall gather the lambs with his arm, and carry them in his bosom, and shall gently lead those that are with young.

"Hast thou not known? hast thou not heard, that the everlasting God, the Lord, the Creator of the ends of the earth, fainteth not, neither is weary? . . . He giveth power to the faint; and to them that have no might he increaseth strength. . . . they that wait upon the Lord shall renew their strength; they shall mount up with wings as eagles; they shall run, and not be weary; and they shall walk, and not faint." (Isaiah 40:9, 11, 28, 29, 31.)

"As the hart panteth after the water brooks, so panteth my soul after thee, O God. . . . Why art thou cast down, O my soul? and why art thou disquieted within me? hope thou in God: for I shall yet praise him, who is the health of my countenance, and my God." (Psalm 42:1, 11.)

"I will lift up mine eyes unto the hills, from whence cometh my help. My help cometh from the Lord, which made heaven and earth. . . . he that keepeth thee will not slumber. The Lord shall preserve thee from all evil: he shall preserve thy soul. The Lord shall preserve thy going out and thy coming in from this time forth, and even for evermore." (Psalm 121:1, 2, 3, 7, 8.)

"In my distress I cried unto the Lord, and he heard me. . . . I am for peace." (Psalm 120:1, 7.)

"O give thanks unto the God of heaven: for his mercy endureth for ever" (Psalm 136:26).

"In the day when I cried thou answeredst me, and strengthenedst me with strength in my soul" (Psalm 138:3).

"Blessed be God, which hath not turned away my prayer, nor his mercy from me" (Psalm 66:20).

"Let thy tender mercies come unto me, that I may live" (Psalm 119:77).

"I will lay me down in peace, and sleep: for thou, Lord, only makest me dwell in safety" (Psalm 4:8).

"The Lord is my light and my salvation; whom shall I fear? the Lord is the strength of my life; of whom shall I be afraid? For in the time of trouble he shall hide me in his pavilion . . . he shall set me up upon a rock. Wait on the Lord: be of good courage, and he shall strengthen thine heart: wait, I say, on the Lord." (Psalm 27:1, 5, 14.)

"The Lord is my shepherd; I shall not want.

"He maketh me to lie down in green pastures: he leadeth me beside the still waters.

"He restoreth my soul: he leadeth me in the paths of righteousness for his name's sake.

"Yea, though I walk through the valley of the shadow of death, I will fear no evil: for thou art with me; thy rod and thy staff they comfort me.

"Thou preparest a table before me in the presence of

mine enemies: thou anointest my head with oil; my cup runneth over.

"Surely goodness and mercy shall follow me all the days of my life: and I will dwell in the house of the Lord for ever." (Psalm 23.)

"Create in me a clean heart, O God; and renew a right spirit within me. Cast me not away from thy presence; and take not thy holy spirit from me. . . . Then will I teach transgressors thy ways; and sinners shall be converted unto thee." (Psalm 51:10, 11, 13.)

"God is our refuge and strength, a very present help in trouble. Be still, and know that I am God." (Psalm 46:1, 10.)

"Be not a witness against thy neighbour without cause; and deceive not with thy lips" (Proverbs 24:28).

"Pleasant words are as an honeycomb, sweet to the soul, and health to the bones" (Proverbs 16:24).

"A word spoken in due season, how good is it! A soft answer turneth away wrath: but grievous words stir up anger." (Proverbs 15:23, 1.)

"I shall not die, but live, and declare the works of the Lord. This is the day which the Lord hath made; we will rejoice and be glad in it. (Psalm 118:17, 24.)

"Thus saith the Lord, Let not the wise man glory in his wisdom, neither let the mighty man glory in his might, let not the rich man glory in his riches: But let him that glorieth glory in this, that he understandeth and knoweth me, that I am the Lord which exercise lovingkindness, judgment, and righteousness, in the earth: for in these things I delight, saith the Lord" (Jeremiah 9:23–24).

"The pleasing word of God, yea, the word which healeth the wounded soul" (Jacob 2:8).

"Because thou hast made the Lord, which is my refuge, even the most High, thy habitation; there shall no evil befall thee, neither shall any plague come nigh thy dwelling. For he shall give his angels charge over thee, to keep thee in all thy ways. They shall bear thee up in their hands, lest thou dash thy foot against a stone." (Psalm 91:9–12.)

Reading the word of God brings peace. There are systems established by great or interested teachers to help us get more out of scripture study. Don't resist the effort of scripture study! Opening the holy books at any place at all and reading the words prepared there is beneficial. Ask yourself why you seek the word of God, and your thoughts will be directed as you look over the pages of tight print holding such truth and inimitable help for all of us, particularly when we are afflicted.

You can look in the concordance, the dictionary, or the index for a subject that interests you at the moment and search these references one at a time.

You can begin with 3 Nephi 11 in the Book of Mormon, which describes Christ's appearance on the American continent after his crucifixion. You can read his fresh teachings to the people here at that time.

You can begin with the New Testament and see what Christ has to say on all manner of subjects—some of which would have special interest to the sick and the afflicted.

You can begin your personal growth in scripture study by finding a set time each day to read the words of God. Regularity brings familiarity and keeps you in tune with God. Then when challenges come in your life or church leadership gives new or different directions, you do not spin your wheels with doubts, complaints, procrastinations, and rationalizations.

Reading the word of God, so pleasing after all and all, can help you compose yourself when you are feeling frazzled and frustrated. Being out of control within yourself is no viable state for problem solving. One of the choice blessings of being an active follower of Christ, one who seeks to keep close to him, is this remarkable sense of self-control, this peace and calm that allows one to function with greater success. New energy comes. Confidence grows. Fear departs. Comfort and well-being wells up while weakness and destructive insecurities seem to melt away.

And all is well. Problems may still exist; sickness, affliction, and temptation may nag at you, but all is well, all is well.

"The grass withereth, the flower fadeth: but the word of our God shall stand for ever" (Isaiah 40:8).

9

Call in
the Elders

any things remind us of God's love for us, and
flowers are high on the list. They speak of a
Master Creator with a plan for man's full joy.

Flowers are God's way of beautifying brown earth, bar-
ren places, and vacant fields. They are a handsome
reminder that he *is* and continues to *be* and kindly creates
relief for our souls in a difficult world. They are a symbol of
life, vitality, and a great outpouring of love.

Across the earth this is true, as with the welcoming
flowers in the handpainted window boxes of Europe; the
delicate, symbolic dogwood blossoms bearing the mark of
the cross and blooming at Easter in the area of Maryland,
Virginia, and the District of Columbia; entire hillsides of
bougainvillea massed in bracts of purple, red, hot pink,
completely surrounding the yacht harbor club on Bain-

bridge Island, Washington; the remarkable sight of acres of cacti, with pink blossoms bursting from their thorny tips following a rare rainstorm in the Arizona desert; the carpet of color from late August wildflowers high in Cedar Breaks, Utah; the last bruised rosebud of fall, its petals sealed with frost; violets under snow covered leaves; and the first brave lawn crocus of spring.

Flowers tell the truth that God is in his heaven, indeed, and all is right with the world no matter what is wrong in our lives. And what is wrong in our lives can be resolved, relieved, restored, or at least assuaged with God's help.

"For, lo, the winter is past, the rain is over and gone; the flowers appear on the earth; the time of the singing of birds is come" (Song of Solomon 2:11–12).

Those inspiring words set the mood for turning a negative into a positive, a yearning into a happening, a hurt into a healing. This happens when we keep ourselves in touch with God and in time of need call upon his servants to be agents unto us for our well-being. This is a plan of love, peace, and security which God has provided for us so that we may learn and progress.

Flowers are symbolic, mood lifters for the sick and afflicted. The elders of the Church also lift us as they are blessed instruments in God's hand for our benefit.

We are not alone!

I recall learning this afresh while meeting extensive Church assignments in the Hawaiian Islands. The schedule was heavy and tight and proved to be so overtaxing that I was stricken with a miserable respiratory infection, accompanied by a high fever. I needed a priesthood blessing if I were to continue my responsibilities. It was arranged for me to meet the elders at the church in advance of a multi-stake mothers and daughters event where I was to speak. The women were coming from far places in great anticipation, and it seemed imperative that I be there, too, to do my part.

In my heart what I really wanted to do was curl up in my hotel bed for one good night's rest. My hostess picked me up at my hotel at an hour far earlier than necessary, I thought, and that didn't help my mood any. I entered the stake center with my shoulders sagging, I must admit, and I was escorted into the cultural hall. What a sweet surprise. The huge hall was crowded with a circle of more than one hundred young women, between the ages of twelve and eighteen, holding exquisite Hawaiian leis made from exotic blooms, fragrant flowers, colorful vines, and fern.

As I walked around the circle to greet each girl, she placed her lei over my head in the affectionate Polynesian tradition. Soon the circles of fresh flowers were layered to my ears. Then my arms were covered from my shoulders to my wrists with leis. With the presentation of each lei the swell of the Spirit increased. There was an amazing outpouring from soul to soul, over and again with each girl.

Unusual leis cost money, energy, trouble, and thought. I knew that parents and daughters, young women and their leaders had discussed this at length. I marvelled at their caring and generous natures. I was humbled as well as delighted. The miracle of love bestowed upon me was so healing to my spirit that, in spite of sickness (even when I was about my Father's business!), by the time I sat under the hands of the elders for an anointing and administration, I was in tune with heaven. I was ready to wait upon the Lord for an appropriate blessing.

And I was healed. My fever lifted, and by the time I was to speak, my voice had returned. I finished the tour in good health and with gratitude.

This experience caused me to think about the importance of being ready for whatever blessing God has in store for us individually when we specifically call in the elders in time of sickness and affliction.

In Christ's day on one occasion, people had thronged to the gate to see the Master enter the Holy City riding on an ass. Palm fronds were laid as a path of honor, and excitement rose high. People pressed the Savior, crowding to be close to him. But there was a woman who had been "diseased with an issue of blood for twelve years." She had spent all she had with doctors and was no better. She "came from behind" the Lord and in faith reached out to touch the hem of his robe, for she had said to herself that if she could but touch his garment, she would be made whole. Such was her faith. Jesus then asked his disciples who had touched him. They pointed out the press of the crowd touching him on all sides. But Jesus knew there was something different about this woman's touch. She had connected. The others merely brushed or pushed, or nudged. But her touch was different. Jesus responded by healing her.

Our touch must be different. We who have sickness, affliction of any kind need to learn how to reach out for the help of God. Calling in the elders to anoint us with consecrated oil and to administer a blessing from God is one of the avenues God has provided for us. This ordinance is most sacred, and we recall that whether the words are uttered by him or his servants it is the same.

There were those privileged to be taught personally by Christ, but for the rest of us he has said something that applies to all God's children for whom "he maketh his sun to rise on the evil and on the good." Jesus said, "Blessed are the poor in spirit [the afflicted] who *come unto me*, for theirs is the kingdom of heaven. And again, blessed are all they that mourn [if we come unto him], for they shall be comforted." (3 Nephi 12:3–4, 45.)

God bless the sick and the afflicted? He does. He will! It is for us to set these holy opportunities in motion.

For example, Lucille had made the brave, long battle with cancer—four years of illness until she reached the terminal stage. The family had endured trauma and trials. In spite of the stress, they had gone about the business of weddings, missions, school activities, and daily chores to keep a family going. Their own illnesses and personal struggles had to be dealt with all the while even as mother's sickness progressed. This meant demanding sacrifice and adjustment. And there was the matter of financial disaster during this period.

Still they loved their valiant wife and mother and were determined to keep her on earth with them. Their prayers pleaded for her life. Their fasting was for her healing. They looked for the miracle still and clung stubbornly to that hope. She was the only woman Mark, her husband, had ever loved, and he simply could not give up Lucille. He couldn't imagine life without her. He wanted *her*, sick or well, but he wanted her alive.

Lucille slipped into a coma, and the doctors knew that the end was nearing. It seemed that only Mark's tenacious faith was holding her here. The strain was telling on him. He sought strength in reading the scriptures and one day read the words in Ether, "Dispute not because ye see not, for ye receive no witness until after the trial of your faith" (Ether 12:6).

As Mark sat pondering these things, it happened that one of the elders of the Church came to the hospital room. Lucille had been given administrations along the path of her illness, but as Mark talked with the wise and experienced elder, he felt prompted to ask for a blessing for himself. He wanted the faith and strength to face whatever was according to God's will. Until that moment Mark had thought that what he himself wanted was right and appropriate. A mother and wife belonged with her family until the children were reared, at least! That was what they had unceasingly prayed for over these long years of affliction.

The ordinance proceeded; hands were placed upon his head. As the flow of words went from earth to heaven through an elder of the Church, Mark listened carefully because he was needful. Then, touched by the Spirit, he relaxed; he turned himself over to God, whom he knew afresh lived and cared about him, about Lucille, about their family. As the administration ended, Mark felt a great burden literally lifted—he felt this physically as well as spiritually. Depression eased and anxiety ceased. He knew what he had to do and he felt right about it, somehow comforted that he was acting in accord with the Lord's purposes.

Mark asked the elder if they now could pray together with Mark being voice. They moved to the bedside of Lucille. Mark knelt there taking in his hand her fragile, listless one, so dear to him. The tears flowed freely as he prayed, but they were not bitter tears this time. They were a result of the outpouring of a contrite and broken heart. He now had the demeanor of a faithful man who trusted that God would want only the best for his children. Mark prayed for God's will to be done and covenanted that he was willing to obey that will, to let go of Lucille and to trust in divine purposes.

Lucille died only minutes later.

Did God bless the sick and afflicted in that instance? Indeed. Let's follow Mark's story down the years after.

Mark was an example to others suffering similar adversity. Mark was a blessing to a new, younger family whom he gathered in through a second marriage. He and Lucille had had only daughters. Now there were sons to help with his business, sons to teach about the priesthood, sons to prepare for missions and good citizenship. And he was a loving husband to a woman who had been deprived of such joy in her life before. He became a trusted leader in the Church himself and proved compassionate to the sufferers and the strugglers and the questioners because of his personal experience. It is important to realize that the power of God rested upon him because of his obedience and his choice to be on the Lord's side.

Grief must have its day. We have been counseled to weep and mourn for those we have loved well. But let us not forget the value of God's counsel that we seek help as he has provided, that we may get on with life, with our individual mission on earth and not waste time unduly in self-pity or adjustment.

I recall with tenderness and appreciation a time when one of the great General Authorities of the Church placed his hands upon our son when his life was at stake. It was a remarkable experience because of the way that high school boy was prepared to receive what the Lord had in store for him.

We were frightened, I admit. This boy had been longed for and prayed for. At last he was born under special circumstances. Now he was high school age, desperately ill, and we didn't want to lose him so soon. (When is there a time that seems right to have our loved ones die?)

After the anointing with consecrated olive oil by another elder, the General Authority became voice to seal the anointing. He addressed Heavenly Father and explained the desires of our hearts, our love of this boy, our faith before God. This was done to put the sick lad in the right frame of mind to receive the blessing. Then this thoughtful elder addressed our son by name and taught him in an inspired and eloquent manner about the plan of life. He called it the "grand adventure" and suggested that the boy fight to keep his spirit alert to some important learning while the body fought in a frightening experience of life threatening affliction. He spelled out some of the lessons and heightened the thinking of us all beyond the hospital room, beyond physical restrictions. We were imbued with hope; more than ever the boy wanted to live for a reason, a purpose. Truths had been brought forth that made life all the more precious and worth fighting for. Our son was imbued with a new will to live.

And then the elder shifted the focus of gears in his

prayer. He addressed the Lord and spoke of the kingdom of God on earth and the great work to be done among men. Here was a lad being prepared to help in the cause. And the plea went forth to flood the sick boy's mind and spirit with understanding of his part in this important work. A witness was given that the will of the Lord was good enough for this family, this teenager. A witness was made that it was known in this family circle that God lived and loved us and his will for us particularly—whether it be life or death at this time for this son—would be the best in the long view. Then came eloquent words of gratitude for life, for learning experiences and the need for obedience and submission to the laws of heaven, for spiritual growth and comfort, for closeness to God and a part in his plan. It was enough. We waited now upon the Lord.

Our son lived through that grueling, sanctifying trial.

We gained an understanding we would not have had without the dreadful threat to this beloved boy's life. It was the trial before our faith was strengthened—one more time.

I share this story here in an effort to trigger in you a remembrance of times when you or your loved ones have been blessed in a similar way.

God bless the sick and afflicted? He did. He has. He will!

A violent traffic accident wreaked havoc in the life of a brilliant and beautiful young mother and professional scientist. She went through long weeks of physical and mental suffering. Head injuries had left her with recurring bouts of deep depression. It was a time of confusion and unhappiness for the whole family. She wasn't a member of the Church and didn't know where to look for help. She had attended seminary with friends during junior high school and had lived a clean life, but now her mighty test had come, and she was ill prepared to meet it appropriately. She was besieged by nameless fears and frustrations.

She tried to pray, to a God whom she remembered again. But nothing seemed to change much. It was determined that she be given psychiatric help. And, interestingly enough, it was with the psychiatrist that she discussed her restless need for some kind of relationship with Deity. The psychiatrist was an active Church member and finally, at the appropriate point, was able to introduce her to the elders. They reminded her of the restored gospel, which she quickly received. At her hesitant, humble request, through the laying on of hands she was given a healing, guiding promise.

Did God bless the sick and afflicted woman? Indeed he did! Later she was baptized and confirmed. Filled with joy, she is grateful for the nightmare she had to endure because of what she has learned, what she feels and knows today. The most important blessings of her life she would not have, she says, if she hadn't paid a price through suffering and sought the help of heaven. Today this family is preparing for the temple experience.

It is customary for the person who is afflicted or someone responsible for that person to request the administration of a blessing. The rest is up to the Lord, for he said, "Whatsoever thing ye shall ask the Father in my name, which is good, in faith believing that ye shall receive, behold, it shall be done unto you" (Moroni 7:26).

The late Elder Bruce R. McConkie wrote, "Ordinances of administration with actual healing resulting therefrom are one of the evidences of the divinity of the Lord's work. Where these are, there is God's kingdom, where these are not, there God's kingdom is not. Sincere investigators must necessarily beware of the devil's substitutes of the true ordinances." (*Mormon Doctrine* [Salt Lake City: Bookcraft, 1966], p. 22.)

There are times when healing doesn't happen in God's church. The beautiful thing to remember is that when we seek God's will during a healing blessing, there comes a flood of comfort and peace, as well as the witness of God's love for those involved, even if the person is not healed or the affliction resolved according to desire.

It is important that when we are sick and afflicted, we *think* about calling upon the elders as our special link with Heavenly Father. It is part of God's plan to bolster our own faith, I believe. In Doctrine and Covenants 42:44 we read, "And the elders of the church, two or more, shall be called, and shall pray for and lay their hands upon them in my name; and if they die they shall die unto me, and if they live they shall live unto me."

We do not know God's timetable or particular purposes for us at any given season. What we do know is that he is a wise and loving, patient and caring Heavenly Father. We are told in Romans 8:16 "The Spirit itself beareth witness with our spirit, that we are the children of God." Wonderful! He has promised us choice blessings if we but abide his will. Therefore, we need to strengthen our faith in these matters, don't we?

Do you recall this perspective in the Doctrine and Covenants: the Lord says he has "suffered the affliction" to come upon his children in consequence of their transgressions. Then he says that they were slow to hearken unto the voice of the Lord their God; therefore, the Lord their God is slow to hearken unto their prayers, to answer them in the day of their trouble. These strong words follow, "Be still and know that I am God." (See Doctrine and Covenants 101:1, 7, 16.)

With God, nothing is impossible. But also, with God, his will must suffice, and we must train ourselves into a degree of faithfulness to accept his will.

For all of us this is precious instruction.

James 5:13–15 gives us the following advice: "Is any among you afflicted? let him pray. . . . Is any sick among you? let him call for the elders of the church; and let them pray over him, anointing him with oil in the name of the Lord: and the prayer of faith shall save the sick, and the Lord shall raise him up; and if he have committed sins, they shall be forgiven him."

Faith is a key. By faith marvelous things can happen. Lives can be saved, changed, motivated, made purposeful, and wonderful works accomplished. By faith Noah built an ark for the saving of his house, and Nephi and the Brother of Jared and their families built ships to cross the great waters to promised lands. By faith Sarah received strength to conceive when she was past the time of women. By faith Abraham took Isaac to the rock as a sacrifice and found a ram in the thicket. By faith Moses refused to be called the son of Pharaoh's daughter but led his people in the Exodus instead, choosing to suffer affliction with the people of God, rather than to enjoy the pleasures of court for a season. By faith the prophets of old and new times have subdued violence, wrought righteousness, obtained promises, survived the den of lions, prophesied of things that were yet unknown but finally fulfilled. By faith Alma and Amulek caused the prison to tumble to the earth. It was by faith that the three Nephite apostles obtained a special promise that they should not taste death. And there were those whose faith was so strong that even before Christ came to earth, they could not be kept from the veil and the vision of how he would be when he did come to dwell among men!

Reading the scriptures to familiarize yourself with the elements of healing in Christ's day should be part of personal preparation when you are considering calling in the elders to receive a blessing. For example, study the "elements of healing" this time, rather than following the narrative. These references, feasted upon, can strengthen your faith and comfort you. We all have moments when we think, "I know God lives. I know he has worked miracles. But a miracle for *me*? How likely is it?"

Being sick and afflicted can put us in a mood to learn, to do, to be, whatever it takes for the healing. The accounts of Christ's miracles as he laid his hands upon—as he *touched*—the sick and afflicted in the land of his birth prove beneficial in and of themselves to most needful people. Begin by studying, feasting, pondering—at least carefully reading—Mark 1:21–45; 3:1–6; 4:35–91; 15:1–43; Luke chapters 4, 5, and 7; Matthew 4.

You will learn that Christ healed both the body and the spirit. You will learn that even unclean spirits of the devil obeyed the Lord's command to the afflicted to be healed. You will learn that the power of God was always *present* in all the healings and miracles. Though at this time, Christ himself isn't among us on earth to command healing, his authorized and ordained servants are. It is simply up to our own personal faith to make the transition from Christ to his elders who are among us and commissioned to do his work among us.

If Christ were to walk through the door of your room now, you would press him for his blessings. Wouldn't you? Don't you believe he could heal and comfort you, even restore you? Of course!

But it doesn't seem to be part of the plan that Christ himself do all the good works. There must be occasion for growth among the holders of the priesthood in serving in such a sacred way and growth in faith among those seeking healing. The power present is what we must come to seek and feel.

Your faith, then, must bridge whatever distance between Christ and his power operating on earth.

Remember that God has told us "if there be no faith among the children of men God can do no miracle among them" (Ether 12:12).

No doubt we can increase our faith by looking again at the world God created for us. It is a place of beauty and order, of incredible variety and marvelous scope. The smallest blossom on its stem or shell at the seashore can remind us of the power of God.

There is a great story about a group of Young Women in a certain stake who took up a project to help the sick and afflicted strengthen their own faith. The girls covered small juice cans with pretty wrapping paper to use as containers for flowers, vines and pods, or colored leaves in season. These were taken to hospitals, nursing homes, children's wards, and to the homes of shut-ins or invalids. Each had a message attached: "Behold this evidence of God's power. Lean upon him."

Flowers, as we said, are symbolic of God's power, and the elders of the Church are blessed instruments in God's hand for our benefit.

10

You Can Take This and More

ragrant lilies of the valley, pansies, and baby's breath draped the mahogany casket. It was being supported on strong straps stretched over the grave opening until after the ground was dedicated and the mourners had moved back to their cars. No longer are people allowed to watch the descent of the deceased into the ground below. The sexton's crew must get on with their work without an audience, it seems.

But I can remember when we did watch the coffin lowered, when we threw in handfuls of soil, tossed in flowers from the funeral sprays, and looked deep into the chasm that would hold the mortal remains of a dearly beloved friend or relative.

Something has been lost in this transition, some part of grieving; some wrapping up of a relationship has been cut off, and we are left with an unfinished symphony, without resolution. We are expected to grow up and take whatever circumstance modern regulations and mores demand.

Once we stood near the newly closed grave of a dear one with the generous floral offerings piled high over freshly mounded soil.

"She is at peace," murmured someone nearby.

I looked at the flowers still softening the ultimate experience in life. And then a strange irreverence flooded me. In my mind I could see a famous *New Yorker* cartoon depicting a sunbather floating on an inflatable pillow in the ocean, contentedly basking in the sunlight. Out of sight, directly beneath him is shown a vicious shark with teeth bared for biting! The caption reads, "Complete peace." Then my thoughts turned back to the deceased said to be at peace.

Beneath the flowers and the six feet of earth is the coffin. In the soil, around and about, are the inevitable worms, beetles, ants, spiders, and the burrowing rabbits, squirrels, and gophers.

"Rest in peace? I hope she does," someone responded.

Another added, "She was ill so long. One needs to be sturdy to die, right?"

And yet another said, "But sturdier to live on, I suppose, especially when life didn't turn out the way she had hoped."

And I wondered, "Does life ever turn out the way you expect?"

It didn't for Jonah!

It didn't for Joseph, sold into Egypt by his brothers, no less.

It didn't for Lot's wife. Nor for Emma.

It didn't for Joseph Smith, either, maligned and martyred.

If you are among the sick and afflicted wondering what slammed into your program, life probably isn't full of the best surprises either. But whatever life brings, you can take this and more. Strengthening your inner spirit, seeking God's help, you can be a survivor like Job. Let's consider some examples:

Sophie helped in our home after she emigrated to America. We could tell by the way she cleaned house that she wasn't a maid by trade; we also could tell that she was a cultured woman with a heavy heart beneath a marvelous smile. As she learned a bit of English and I caught on to her German, we came to know each other better and value each other. I was years younger than Sophie. We had quite different backgrounds. Still we found much to share and laugh about.

We wept together, too, because life certainly wasn't what Sophie had planned. She was half Jewish and had been caught in the Nazi era. Her twin daughters had been separated from her and from each other for twenty miserable years. They were still little children when she was taken to a concentration camp without so much as a good-bye or any inkling of what would become of them. Her long song to us was to value our togetherness as a family. She couldn't abide the smallest quarrel that normal, lively children such as ours might engage in.

Sophie knew what pain family separation brought. Our children didn't. Experience is an effective teacher.

"How can you stand it," I would ask again and again.

"The passing of time, good new relationships, peaceful country . . . these things help," she would reply.

"But Sophie, your very own children. Not to know where they are. Twins!" And I'd hug my baby close.

"I have seen people terribly tortured and worse for no reason. I'm all right. I can take this and more," she inevitably added before biting her lips.

Sophie's life in America was never easy, either. Nothing for her was like it was before World War II in Europe. The work she was forced to do not only brought in insufficient income, but she felt it was demeaning. People were kind, but the nights were long with painful, dark hours to think about the past and worry about her next meal. However, her constant goal was not to burden herself or others with her problems. Whatever life was, it was to be lived and learned from.

I learned from Sophie. And from Charles.

Charles spoke with calmness of spirit; only on occasion did his voice break, revealing the deep emotion that remembering stirred. He always had been a religious man, willing to serve, anxious to grow in understanding of the gospel. He had traditional lofty plans for his life. They didn't work out.

When Charles married, there followed years of deplorable experiences. The relationship was like nothing he ever could have imagined. His wife would not have children. She would not allow him to touch her, and finally she turned into a dangerous neurotic. Then came the years of her repeated attempts at suicide and midnight rides to the emergency ward; the embarrassment in front of neighbors when the rescue squads showed up midday at their home.

He was publicly—deliberately—humiliated by this woman. His own family was estranged because of her. He could not institutionalize her. He had made a commitment for eternity. Divorce was not an option. The way he survived the stress and unhappiness was to turn to God. This he did on a daily basis, pleading for strength to endure, to cope. With the Lord's help he did endure. He did cope. But he admits that he prayed for the better part of twenty-five years for this bitter cup to pass.

Then one day at last, the nightmare was over. She was dead and he was free. He was grey haired, a little stooped, and surely past his prime, but he was free. And he had learned that he could take whatever life demanded without caving in.

Charles retired and moved to a small city and found part-time work as a salesman in a hardware store. Because he had kept close to the Lord all these years, he had not allowed himself to become bitter or complaining. He became a man who understood people, a man of great compassion for what others might be suffering or what they might be concealing. He devoted his days to spreading the joy people sorely need in our time.

Then one day a brown-eyed girl with a warm smile took hold of Charles' hand and heart. They were married quickly, and Margaret gave him the love he'd never known. Blessings flowed into their lives and from them into the lives of others.

Three short years later Charles stood at this beloved wife's funeral and shared his story with us. He was emotionally devastated, and yet he emphasized, "I can take this sad turn of events and more because of my long years of trust in Christ."

Charles bore a fervent testimony that God heard the prayers of the sick and afflicted. He felt the sure promise that there would yet be joy and hope and a future for Margaret and him. Theirs was an eternal, loving relationship. God had brought them together once and would again. Meanwhile, endure loneliness. Endure bread when you had tasted cake. But keep close to God.

The Olympic events bring forth some interesting details about the athletes. Many are inspiring for us in our various life situations. *Newsweek* magazine (September 19, 1988, p. 55) featured a cover picture of Florence Griffith Joyner. The story of the super sprinter included from her mother a statement of belief which bears consideration for our subject here.

When Flo-Jo was four, her mother took her eleven children away from their dad in the Mojave Desert and moved them into a four bedroom apartment in a housing project in Watts—the scene of the infamous Watts riots. She had thirty cents in change to begin the new life. But it was a well-ordered life for these children based on Bible study and strict rules, including no weeknight television or carousing. The mother explained to the children that life was "like a baby. A baby comes into the world without anything. Then it starts crawling; then it stands up. Then it takes its first step and starts walking. When we moved into the project I told them, 'Start walking.' "

Flo-Jo took the advice and fought her way through the tough life of Watts. She did her rigorous physical training after a full day's work to become a national celebrity and the fastest woman who ever ran 100 meters. She lifts and reaches when she runs and as she lives. She is admired for her attitude of "I can overcome. I can take this and more, but I will succeed."

John Smith participated in the Munich Olympic events some years ago. His story was a heartbreaker, too. After incredible sacrifice and struggle he qualified for the USA team. He started the 400 meter event and was barely into it when his face contorted. He'd pulled a hamstring, and his career ended. John gave lectures to motivate people not to give up if life hands you a heartbreak. Afflictions can become blessings. There are others things to do, other things to feel, other goals to set.

"I turned this negative into a positive. I came home and got a job at UCLA as a coach," explained Smith. And he was a trainer for the 1988 Olympic track events.

The long way "home" is living until you die, people like this emphasize.

Christmas cards painted by the handicapped have always impressed me. Imagine wanting to paint so much that you'd learn to do it holding the brush in your mouth or with your toes! Imagine earning your livelihood that way. I buy the sets of boxed cards painted by such brave souls and send them forth with pride, wonder, and as an example of victory.

Dorothy Stowe in a bylined article in the *Church News* reported on the courage of Karen Rigby of Surrey Downs, South Australia. Life didn't turn out to be what she had in mind, either, but God has blessed her in her affliction. She has persevered as an artist and found satisfaction in helping visually impaired, legally blind students learn to paint. "None of them has given up, and no one has gone away," said Karen. Her method includes a paint she invented which has a raised texture that makes it easier for the blind to use and have success with. But the real force in her success is attitude.

Karen is one of those who believe "I can take this and more because I already have taken so much; because I understand principles of living life with God's help."

Affliction comes in different forms. Sometimes we are innocent victims like Jim Brady, who was shot during the assassination attempt on President Ronald Reagan in March 1981. The havoc those bullets inflicted was awful and frightening. Brady's brain was penetrated, and though few people survive such damage, Jim Brady did. With help from God and loved ones, he has not only survived, he has embarked again on life's journey among the living away from hospital and care centers toward a victorious triumph.

"You have to persevere. Persevere and keep your sense of humor. They can't shoot that away," insists Brady.

According to therapists, medical personnel, and loved ones who support him, Brady is never, never willing to quit. He insists he can take all the pain, the mental and physical anguish his situation requires—and more if need be. He isn't in the battle for himself alone. He has made his contribution far beyond that of ordinary people by helping older and younger victims of stroke, accident, or other aspects of personal assault.

Can we do less?

With what we know and understand about God and

the plan of life, with what we learn from the examples of others, with what we at last come to appreciate about our own inner resources, can't we then "take this" and more?

In every household of faith, sooner or later, regularly or rarely comes the wrenching test. The heart of a tender wife is broken because her husband is an adulterer. The aching of a soul robs sleep as fear fashions dreams of death. Long hours of counseling together eats into the lives of a family with a teenager addicted to chemical substances. Shame sickens the household as public disgrace follows poor business choices. Tears upon tears flow easily in the wake of loneliness night after night. Horror engulfs loved ones as out of surprise corners come the calamities. A headache is diagnosed as cancer. The wrestle with evil forces, the bouts with depression, the struggle for serenity in stressful relationships, the search for sustaining faith and courage must be endured. O the burdens of the sick and the afflicted.

There are three good truths to remember:

1. You know some things about affliction because of the fulness of the gospel. You know that some of your troubles are your own fault; some are part of God's plan. Some are the work of the devil. Some are simply circumstance, rendering you a hapless victim.

As for the devil, C. S. Lewis in his book *The Great Divorce* declares there can be no compromise. The battle of life is to escape from Satan's influence. On the title page of that book, Lewis uses an intriguing quote from George McDonald. "There is no heaven with a little of hell in it — no plan to retain this or that of the devil in our hearts or pockets. Out Satan must go, every hair and feather."

2. You don't have to solve all of your own problems. The Lord's arms are forever outstretched for you. His powers hover over you always but he waits for you to *allow* him (remember your free agency?) to be gracious in special

ways. He has said that you should cast your burdens upon him. He has said that we are to become as he is. And we can, through trials well-endured.

His wisdom is available to us in this endeavor. His word tells us "all things that we must do." If we don't know His word, we cannot live by it.

One of the most blatant misconceptions among people is the assumption that because they don't "drink or smoke, etc." they are automatically well-rooted in gospel doctrine. Or they think that because they are holders of a temple recommend and a church position, or pay tithes, for example, that they *know* God's deep and saving doctrine. It simply isn't so. They only think they know the word of God, but they do not! They may know *some* of the word of God, but their lives indicate areas of ignorance. Their lives prove otherwise.

To know is to be converted, which is to do! Faith without works won't work. Prayer without knowledge of and application of eternal principles in the fine detail can be comforting but not conclusive.

3. Think of your best moments. Give yourself credit for sustaining the family, or hiding your hurt, or enduring humiliation, or sacrificing self for others—whatever. Remind yourself that in your *best* moments you are *not* full of iniquity, jealous of a friend, untrusting of a spouse, lacking in reverence, thankless for blessings, impatient for the perfection of everyone else, angry at God.

Now grow up again, and be your best in your worst moments. Anything less leaves you vulnerable to the adversary.

4. You *can* endure and cope when affliction hits. Your inner reserves can be drawn upon to help because you are a quality person. A firm mental set is the secret. For example, repeat such phrases as these: "I suffer and endure." "I *can* hurt and not cry." "I can stand being ig-

nored and forgotten and lonely." "I can fast." "I can forgive." "I can say I am sorry." "I can live on a lower income." "I can bring order out of chaos." "I can take this and more."

The difference in people is evident as you watch them deal with their goals and desires as well as their afflictions. How badly do they want to endure positively the vicissitudes of life? How badly do they want to be an example of the believer in Christ?

How badly do you want to be patient, creative, financially solvent, healthy, rich, a scriptural scholar, a compassionate friend, a loving priesthood leader, a responsive spouse, an unselfish parent, a loyal neighbor?

Mediocre people abound. What we need are people who will take a stand. We need fellow sufferers who can take it without whining.

11

Little Moments
of Beauty

 ow quaint a picture the flower vendor made! The cart itself spilled over with bachelor buttons, ranunculuses, African daisies, gardenias, snapdragons, roses, carnations, heather, violets, gladioli and chrysanthemums. The flower stall was fanciful with its multicolored bric-a-brac. The genial seller of beauty and fragrance had his beret cocked over one eye and his lips pursed into a whistle. Obviously he was happy in his work.

This picture was in a travel brochure, and the enticing sales pitch for a future vacation said, "Little moments of beauty like this are apt to pop up everywhere in Europe."

Actually, little moments of beauty are apt to pop up anywhere at all in life, too. They are a valuable perk. If we'll but look for them, we'll find them, even in the midst of trouble and despair.

This personal experience may prove the point. One bleak January our family came home from a long-weekend trip and found water seeping down the basement walls and puddling the floor below. The record-breaking zero temperatures had turned the seepage into tiny sheets of ice wherever the water had traveled.

Naturally my husband and I were horrified. The children, however, quickly squealed in delight at frozen patterns marking the concrete and unfamiliar icicles clinging to the rough sides of the unfinished basement walls.

"It's a frost garden," laughed four-year-old Susan. "Jack Frost has been here. He's been inside our very house. Look!"

Our little artist went scurrying to examine, and point out to the rest of us, the "frost garden" flowers, ferns, and spikes.

Susan saw the beauty. I saw that these frozen designs were splitting the concrete, sogging the carpet, matting the stuffed animals of the play area, and inevitably creating more work for Mother and Dad.

But to see beauty in a time of trauma stimulates hope for better times.

It's easy to see beauty in the stretch of pink blooms of a peach orchard in early spring. But to see chic monochromatic beauty instead of boring sameness as one looks across a winter field, snow drifted against the beige stakes of a barbed wire fence and beyond, the beige nakedness of poplars marking the border from mountain to highway, it takes quite another sort of eye—and heart. How much better it is for one's disposition to be such a beholder of beauty.

Applied to the times of affliction in our lives, we can soften our suffering if we search for the good and, yes, the beautiful in a time of sickness and affliction.

The fresh flower auction on the outskirts of Amsterdam is an overwhelming experience in this perspective. There in a cavernous metal warehouse both views are possible. The catwalk above the auction floor allows the visitor to view vast acreage of fresh, cut, florist-ready blooms or else the intricate superstructure of the warehouse ceiling. It all depends on what one is looking for. I wasn't interested in structural steel, so I looked at the incredible quantity and variety of flowers below.

For me it was just a hint of being a God to survey from high up those thousands of carts massed with tulips, iris, jonquils, roses, statice, carnations (and more) in every elegant color in all its shadings. It was a living oriental carpet as far as the eye could see. The paisley pattern shifted as the carts were wheeled in and out of the auction rooms. The enormous living, blooming rug changed before our eyes like a kaleidoscope working its magic.

Taking the long, wide, distant view of the proceedings at the flower auction, as a visiting tourist usually does, one sees beauty. The workers on the warehouse floor, however, concentrate on flaws. Busily they scan every bouquet and bundle, every blossom and blade for imperfection. Swiftly they sort out and discard bruised blooms, withered stems, and wilted leaves.

And therein lies a message.

When, for the time being, you are counted among the sick and the afflicted—the wilted, withered times of life, if you will—there surely is some pruning, some plucking, some sifting and trashing to do. This proves beneficial. Clue: notice how much better you feel when your negative memories are discarded, and the beautiful moments are remembered.

God has blessed us with flowers that come up in season no matter what scourge mankind has initiated on the earth.

God has blessed us with an ocean that roars its white-capped power to out-sound the systems of war wherever they might be. The ebb and flow of the tide can be counted on whatever else changes on the face of the earth.

God has created man with the ability to reason and the agency to choose whether we will pursue moments of beauty or dwell upon being sick and afflicted, treasuring up negative incidents.

These familiar lines from *Life's Mirror* by Madeline S. Bridges are relevant.

> There are loyal hearts, there are spirits brave,
> There are souls that are pure and true;
> Then give to the world the best you have,
> And the best will come back to you.
>
> Give love, and love to your life will flow,
> A strength in your utmost need;
> Have faith, and a score of hearts will show
> Their faith in your word and deed.
>
> Give truth, and your gift will be paid in kind,
> And honor will honor meet;
> And a smile that is sweet will surely find
> A smile that is just as sweet.
>
> Give sorrow and pity to those who mourn;
> You will gather in flowers again
> The scattered seeds of your thought
>   outborne,
> Though the sowing seemed but vain.
>
> For life is the mirror of king and slave—
> 'Tis just what we are and do;
> Then give to the world the best you have,
> And the best will come back to you.

Being among the sick and afflicted has a way of short-circuiting your power to think about anything else at all except yourself. Haven't you noticed this? However, since it is better to feel better than to feel worse, it is worth the effort to trash the negative moments in life. Deal with them, of course, but almost in a never-let-the-left-hand-know-what-the-right-hand-is-doing sort of thing. It is almost like brushing off a pesky fly with an automatic wave of the hand while moving on to important things in life.

Consider the following ways to get on with the beautiful moments:

1. *Remind yourself of the best of times*

Look at old pictures, journals, memorabilia, year-books, treasures from a happier time or another set of circumstances. Unfold old table linen and remember special gatherings. Rearrange holiday decor in the storage area and allow the flood of dear friends and loved ones with whom you celebrated to cross your heart. Take out the baby books, the files of clippings and primitive art saved for a child. Why happy days are here again in an instant, if only for an instant, but then healing can begin.

2. *Take a mini-trip*

Get away from it all. While Europe in living color may not be a possibility under "sick and afflicted" status, waft yourself off to Greece or the Panama by browsing through coffee table picture books of exotic places. The public library has a rich supply. Even the old hometown holds plenty of possibilities for diversion. Get your mind off your trouble for a time by going to see urban renewal projects, block renovations, historic restorations, gardens in seasonal bloom, or winter wonderlands after a fresh snowfall.

3. *Gift wrap moments of beauty*

Whenever you can, turn a beautiful moment into a memory you can draw on later when you need to stifle a bad day. Do it with a camera. Record it in your diary. Talk it into your recorder. Press a flower. Tell a friend. Thank God in prayer.

I am thinking of the way one brave family found beauty in heartbreak. The son was preparing for a mission, but those plans were changed when he was hit by a truck while riding his motorcycle. He was left paralyzed from his shoulders down and with brain damage. He is cared for at home now. Though he will never be as he once was, still careful effort is made by the family to ease his situation. Even the planning to fulfill this goal has helped to ease things for the family. It puts the focus on activity instead of grief. Everyday the invalid gets fresh flowers or an interesting *objet d'art* on his food tray. For the main meal he is served on china. Candles burn for a festive air, and a cloth napkin adds class. Soft music awakens him in the morning. All of this adds luster to the grim routine of the patient, and it stretches the creative skills of the caregiver.

Our neighbor Victoria Troxler saw to it on a daily basis that her sister, Allie, a crippling arthritis victim, had clean, carefully ironed, hand-embroidered pillowcases with a bright edge of hand-crocheted lace. This meant four or five clean cases a day because Allie's arms, knees and back, as well as her head, were supported by pillows. A bottle of scented lotion was always on her table to use in the event of visitors. She was sick and afflicted, but life had its beautiful moments.

4. *Change your routine*

If you are weeping, put on a video comedy or give *Reader's Digest*'s "Laughter, the Best Medicine" section a more thorough reading. And laugh. Eat your pie before your potatoes. Put on drop earrings instead of studs. Tie on a bow instead of a Windsor. Send yourself some flowers—the surprise comes when you see exactly what the florist delivers. Borrow your son's sweater and feel seventeen again. Take the phone off the hook, fill the tub with therapeutic suds, and soak to the strains of Vivaldi on the stereo. Yes, these activities sound contrived, but they are deliberate diversion tactics that can change your mood from self-pity to self-sustaining.

5. *Remember who you really are*

Search your genealogy or your family history book. As you become reacquainted with your heritage, you'll note there have been important precedents set. Those proud, strong ancestors of yours suffered some, too, in their day and time and circumstance.

6. *Bridle all your passions that you may be filled with love*

That is a choice scripture and good advice in finding moments of beauty. Love breeds moments of beauty. All the good feelings God has made possible for us in our best moments cannot be enjoyed if we choose to see and feel, mark and dwell upon the negative. To me, bridling passions suggests controlling the tendencies to self-pity, grief, anger, jealousy, lust, low self-esteem, hate and envy, impatience and unrest. If you can bridle your passions, life ought to be more beautiful!

7. *Pay attention to life's moments of beauty*

Emotional security comes with positive input. Dealing with affliction then can be accomplished with a refreshed spirit, a clearer mind, a heartened will, a firmer resolve.

Pollyanna-ism can be good for you, too!

In his book *How to Live 365 Days a Year*, John A. Schindler, M.D., reports on a patient of his who had to be hospitalized with an emotionally induced illness. Dr. Schindler wrote, "Her underlying trouble was that she had become thoroughly dissatisfied with everything in her life. She had been educated in an excellent eastern school to be a secretary and had a wonderful position in Washington, D.C. when World War II came along and brought a certain young, handsome army captain in and out of the office in which she worked.

"One and one add up to four—I mean two, at first—they were married and had two children by the time the war was over, over, that is, for everyone but a woman named Ellen. Then she found herself living in a trailer, bringing up her children in a trailer (soon there were three).

"The first time I was called to see her, she was in bed at one end of the trailer, and the captain stood wringing his hands at the other end. She told me, in no uncertain terms and in a voice that made the captain's fingers white, that she didn't like housekeeping and she didn't like living in a trailer, or keeping house in a trailer, and bringing up children in a trailer was terrible . . . and she certainly wished she had stuck to her secretary's job in Washington.

"I was sure, from other remarks, she was dissatisfied with her physician (me!) since he wasn't getting her over her nausea and dizziness. She welcomed the idea of the hospital for the simple reason it took her out of that so-and-so trailer. Without giving her a diagnosis, I ordered her (we were past the suggesting stage) to send to the library for the four Pollyanna books they had.

"Now, many people may consider them silly books, but usually the people who call them silly are on the defensive because of a rotten disposition, and they halfway know it. Anyway, the young lady read the books. I didn't say a thing; at the moment, she was enjoying the hospital.

"One morning she volunteered her own diagnosis. I had known all along she was bright enough. She said, 'I've been thinking . . . what a little fool I am. . . . I can't change my situation, at least not right away. You and Pollyanna win; what am I making myself miserable for?'

"You see, she had the idea, the simple idea, that it's easier to be satisfied than dissatisfied, and much healthier. She read the Pollyanna books . . . she quickly learned the art of being satisfied. She evolved her own little mental tricks and had a lot of fun doing it. It wasn't long before she was perfectly well . . . as I say, she really had a great deal of good sense.'' (From the book *How to Live 365 Days a Year*, by John A. Schindler, M.D. Copyright © 1954. Used by permission of the publisher, Prentice-Hall, Inc., Englewood Cliffs, NJ.)

It is also easier to find moments of beauty than to cultivate one's afflictions!

8. *Say the good word*

Instead of battling with yourself over your failures, over persisting bad habits, make it a new habit to say the good word. Talk the positive talk. Think the happy thought—it is in there within you someplace.

Hardly any moment in life couldn't be improved by a little humor, a cheerful lift, a brave resolve, a verbal toss to prove there is more than trouble in this grand adventure.

9. *Reach out to others*

Forget yourself by reaching out to others. You know the scriptural command ''Lose your life to find it.'' Try this experiment and prove it yourself because it works, according to thousands of other troubled people who have. In John 12:24–25 it says, ''Except a corn of wheat fall into the ground and die, it abideth alone: but if it die, it bringeth forth much fruit. He that loveth his life shall lose it; and he that hateth his life in this world shall keep it unto life eternal.''

Another way of saying it is to bloom where you are planted, like the home or Relief Society crafted articles frequently proclaim.

10. *Cultivate the Holy Spirit*

In Doctrine and Covenants 130:23 we read that a person may receive the Holy Ghost, and it may even descend upon him or her and not tarry. That is a startling and revealing truth. Unless we cultivate the Spirit (using the word cultivate in its sense of ''to foster the growth of'') the

Spirit cannot dwell within us. Then we have lost one of the most effective forces against affliction. We do not automatically, forever, and under all circumstances qualify for the constant companionship of the Holy Ghost, just as we will not automatically dwell with God in his heaven unless we are pure, for no unclean thing can enter the kingdom of heaven and the Holy Ghost cannot dwell in any unclean, disobedient being.

As you seek to lay hold on every good thing, to find moments of beauty, to remain valiant and faithful through all and all, to look for rainbows in storms, if you will, you will find that you can deal with affliction with a refreshed spirit, a clearer mind, a heartened will, a firmer resolve. And with the accompaniment of the Holy Spirit!

Remember the flower vendor in the travel ad for Europe? Well, lovely though it might be for a fantasy, you'll never be satisfied with a picture from a travel brochure as a "little moment of beauty." Life offers us more than that. Go for it!

12

It's All in Your Perspective

ow I recall from my youth a fine teacher at church who brought a bucket—not a vase or basket—to the class as a visual aid. It was filled with a variety of flowers from her famous "grandmother's garden" as she called it. As the lesson unfolded, each flower was likened to one of us in the class. Each different. Each lovely in its way. Each offering a dimension on beauty that any other flower simply couldn't meet. Black-eyed Susans, nasturtium, snapdragons, tea roses, show roses, old-fashioned climbers, hollyhocks, delphinium, pansies, snowballs, marigolds, forget-me-nots, lilies of the valley, and so on. Then she explained that it wasn't the container that counted (hence the bucket and not a basket); it was the essence of beauty of each flower itself.

It was an important lesson for us girls. There were four or five of us in the class who were live wires, up to our hair

111

ribbons in school activities and Church opportunities, all the while tirelessly talking about boys and parties to get us together. There were a couple of nice girls who didn't quite fit in with the group, but still had their own kind of fun. And there was the girl, a late arrival in a family with older parents and married sisters, who was absolutely out of it—in the way she looked and lived, at least. If ever a class needed the lesson, it was this one. The live wires needed it for one reason, and the loner needed it for another. And we learned it.

All through life flowers—and even God's vegetables—can remind us of the beauty and value in variety. If we get cocky or if we are depressed with ourselves, we can take stock, find a proper perspective and move forward with what we came down on earth to do. We can learn, prepare, perform, and pray in thanksgiving as well as for help. God's guidance is imperative.

Have you ever walked resolutely up the stairs or into the next room and suddenly realized that you can't recall why you are there or for what you came? The purpose of that little trip escaped you completely, at least for the moment. So you have to stop and work it through or retrace your steps until, with a flash, understanding comes.

Life is like that for some of God's children all of their days. They don't ever seem to know what the trip to earth was for. Their timing in life is off. They play like they are married when they are not. Or they behave as if they are not married when they in fact are! They learn social graces after they've committed the social blunder. They turn to Heavenly Father only when they are in dire difficulty instead of keeping close to him right along.

Sometimes others of us, who came to earth toting along our particular bag of talents, may stop during periods of pressure and find ourselves at the top of the stairs, so to speak, momentarily at a loss for understanding. Life can be like that on occasions, particularly if we are counted among the sick and afflicted in some way.

You may ask yourself certain questions and ache for answers. Why do I feel so threatened? Why am I ill, stricken this way, now? Why am I running so fast? Why do I find myself in certain situations obediently carrying out a call or living a heartbreak? Why am I hurting? Why do I have to go through *this*? Why am I painfully restless? Why has God forgotten me?

In spite of the questions that seem to have only vague answers, if any, there are times when you must do what you must do, whether you understand at the moment or not. This was, after all, Abraham's predicament wasn't it? And Emma's?

On other occasions, there are some golden moments of real clarity for you, when you know who you are. You may even have an inkling of what it is that you are to be about.

For instance, you will hear the prophet speak, or the scriptures suddenly come alive, or you'll read your patriarchal blessing afresh, or you will have an experience accompanied by a flash of insight, a new perspective on life for you—as differentiated from life for anybody else. . . .

"O, I see, this is why I came to Baltimore!"

"So this is why I married John" (or perhaps, why I didn't).

"Ah, and if my husband hadn't died so young and left me to support the family, I'd never have gone back to school. I wouldn't have learned what I've learned, been able to help as I have helped."

"I'd never have guessed the real reason for being called to this position. Now I see!"

When the light of understanding fills your being, you get a perspective about life that is valuable. Your turn on earth takes on new importance, and is more directed. You feel part of the grand plan. You sense your own worth and heaven's caring.

But if you limp along through life without ever grasping this, if the gospel of Jesus Christ has not touched your life sufficiently to bless you with this perception of the scheme of things, surely you have missed the whole point of life itself.

Consider this ludicrous example. What if an Olympic swimmer showed up at poolside in football padding, carrying a tennis racquet, and adjusting his hard hat? Sticking from his pocket is a booklet of rules for the game—not of swimming, football or tennis but, of all things, chess?

Wrong perspective makes poor preparation for performance.

Yet sometimes you handle your precious life, your one chance on earth, in just such a confused fashion. But there is no need to be like the mythical mixed-up athlete. Heavenly Father, who gave you life, gave clear guidelines and saving principles to live it with. One learns the rules and follows them. Ideally speaking, that is.

The right perspective makes all the difference. The right perspective provides hope. There is a basic statement from the Lord on this matter that can provide each of us with a personal perspective about our choices in life. It is found in section 130 of the Doctrine and Covenants, among other excellent guidelines found in this remarkable section of truth. "There is a law, irrevocably decreed in heaven before the foundations of this world, upon which all blessings are predicated—and when we obtain any blessing from God, it is by obedience to that law upon which it is predicated" (D&C 130:20–21).

So if we want a certain blessing, we must live the law. If we want a warm marriage or a quiet conscience, we apply the laws or principles to life that assure us that our homes will be places of abiding affection and our hearts full of peace instead of regrets.

With this perspective, life can be an amazing adventure, whatever comes our way. We have a game plan. We have sure direction.

For example, a fine LDS couple who had presided over a mission and had always held positions of leading other people, both in the Church and in the financial sector, became aware that, while they had been busy in their lives, their children, who had married and were moving in their own sphere, seemed to have faulty perspective in some instances. Early one morning, after a sleepless night of worry and prayer, the father arose and composed the following letter which he sent to each offspring. I include it here with his permission and for your benefit. There is a precedent for such strong and loving action in the Book of Mormon, in Alma chapters 36 through 42 when Alma calls each of his sons to him and individually teaches them the "things pertaining to righteousness."

"An open letter to the family:

"Mother and I are deeply concerned with what we see happening in our family. In fact, we are very disappointed with the apparent total disregard for putting 'first things first' in your marriage and homes.

"Your first responsibility is to your companion—not your vocation, or ego, or children, or any other facet of life. It is simply a matter of selfishness on the part of one party or the other when we destroy our former love by neglect and inconsideration for each other.

"Life for all is complex and demanding. Your children were brought into this world by *your* choice, not theirs. You have a sacred responsibility for their welfare and training. When they see conflict and lack of love and even tears or sorrow caused by the actions of one spouse or the other, it just isn't right. This 'time and all eternity covenant' that you two entered into with each other and God is sacred. It was meant for your happiness.

"Sure, you can point fingers, but are you big enough to accept your own shortcomings? Are you a worthy father? An exemplary priesthood holder? A loving and considerate companion? Or are you the 'king of the walk'?

"As a mother, do you hold your husband up to the children? Do you set a spiritual and a loving atmosphere in the home?

"*Remember, this is a joint venture!* It is more important than how much money you make or what kind of car you drive or how big your Christmas is. Or anything else.

"As your parents, we paid our price for rearing our children. We set a good example. We were unselfish. We balanced the spiritual and temporal and social dimensions of life. You can, too, if you try to forget yourself and be concerned for your companion and family first.

"Mother and I can't solve your problems. They are created by you yourselves and can only be solved by yourselves. We can support and encourage, but our role now is not that of full-time counselor and referee. We don't know how much time we will continue to enjoy good health and well-being. I am still the patriarch in the family and deeply care what happens to each of you, but it is impossible for Mother or me to take on the family responsibilities for our eight children and our numerous grandchildren. It seems to me that we should be entitled to some happiness and peace of mind from the family.

"President McKay said 'No amount of success can compensate for failure in the home.' Each of you ask yourself, 'Am I failing in the home?'

"*What can you do?*

"One: Put your companion first. Take time out for each other.

"Two: Be concerned about your children and help build a loving environment with family prayer, family home evening, temple attendance and scripture reading.

"Three: Learn to say, 'I am sorry. I will try to do better.'

"Four: Put your family responsibilities where they belong—first in your life. FIRST!

"Fifth: Never forget that we love you and that God loves you.

"Mother and Dad

"P.S. This is Cinderella counsel—if the shoe fits, wear it!"

The father cared. The children responded appropriately. That was one letter worth writing.

With gospel perspective we enjoy all kinds of hope even though we may be locked into difficult situations at the moment.

Consider this beautiful promise from God that comes to you when you have tried to keep his counsel: "For by doing these things the gates of hell shall not prevail against you; yea, and the Lord God will disperse the powers of darkness from before you, and cause the heavens to shake for your good . . ." (D&C 21:6).

How powerful are these promises for the struggling young father trying to provide for his family in these competitive, costly days. The Lord will cause the heavens to shake for your good! To the depressed and lonely unmarried girl or forgotten widow—the Lord God will disperse the powers of darkness from before you! Well, all right! Onward and upward!

Our personal worth, our essence of human dignity is not so much in what we accomplish as in what we come to understand. For proof of this, we need only to look at the troubled, hopeless lives around us. People who do not know the Lord and his laws irrevocably decreed that bring forth golden blessings—such people do not have the proper perspective of the purpose of life. And it shows.

But you do.

If you'll live as if you have this perspective, and not live just as the world lives, then when you get to the top of the stairs—proverbial gold stairs this time—you'll know why you are there. All the promises of God will be fulfilled for you.

I know this.

Remember that the Lord sustains you in your sickness and affliction, in your struggles—not because you are perfect but because he is. He loves you, and he has an endless capacity to love. Surely this perspective should turn you to him in greater devotion and to learning and living his principles.

The teacher in my youth who brought the bucket of flowers to our class helped me understand that each of us is different, but each is valuable. Not only is each of us of worth before God, but each of us has a particular mission to perform on earth. And there is a time and a season to be about our father's particular business. This perspective of God, man, and the plan of life has proved a blessing to me at every stage: youth, young adult, young married, during the season of real service, and grandmother.

May it prove so to you.

13

In the Midst of Affliction

he daisy, by the shadow that it casts, protects the lingering dew drop from the sun,'' wrote William Wordsworth. Affliction can perform a similar service for us.

When President Hugh B. Brown made one of his last appearances before a general conference, he was helped to the pulpit and bodily supported while he spoke. His skin was as white as the parade of lilies banking the balustrades of the great Salt Lake Tabernacle. This beloved giant, physically and spiritually, had won our hearts down through the years. This seemed an even greater moment of example from him and learning for us. Even with all the principles we had learned from his fine mind and sensitive soul over the years of his public service, this day the truth seemed more relevant.

He said at once that he was grateful for all of the experiences of life—including the recent physical trials he'd had to endure. Then he added that most of these experiences he would have chosen to forego if he'd had anything to say about it.

Still, he said he was grateful for them. And the congregation laughed in understanding.

How true that is! For example, surely you wouldn't deliberately walk out and be hit by a truck, expose yourself to a dread disease, sink your money into a sure-failure scheme, or have twins when you are over forty and already parents of eight other children, just to gain experience. What President Brown was pointing out was that when trouble does slam you, if you can find a way to endure it, even to somehow flourish under it, then you can look back in gratitude to God that your strength did not slacken under it.

I care that you are stricken and suffering, if that's your lot at this time. Surely all around you are people who love you and ache for you and are willing to be cheerleaders for your endurance test. We pray that you remember this and find the will to not lose faith or perspective.

During a recent Primary presentation I sat as a tender grandmother watching the beautiful royal generation born that much closer to the second coming of Christ. What a choice, bright lot they are. And the six-year-old blonde beauty on the front row was one of the best. She was our granddaughter! I watched Catherine's face and could easily hear her strong, true voice above the rest as she sang out "God can count on me." I knew she meant it. And I was just as sure that God could always count on her, such character shown forth from her then. I thrilled that she sang it with understanding, if a fervent punctuation of words was any indication.

In that instant I felt rejuvenated as well as tutored. I wanted to be that fresh in my faith, that hopeful that I could conquer and stand and be counted on as among the strong and valiant ones. In my heart I prayed I'd feel that way right to the grave. Of course, Catherine is beginning. Some might suggest, "She doesn't know the half of it, or she wouldn't sing about such impossibilities!" But isn't everything relevant? Doesn't life offer its grim realities as well as its sweet surprises all along the way, and don't we have to react appropriately at each stage in order to move on to the next?

Of course. So Catherine remains a fresh example.

Back to President Brown. I recall the sage who leaned into my ear after President Brown finished speaking at that particular conference and whispered: "Life is like a grindstone. Whether it polishes you up or grinds you down depends on the stuff you're made of."

Therein lies the challenge. And perhaps the question of Catherine. We may not be certain what our point of no return is or how much we can take. We need to prepare ahead to stand strong at any given challenge or affliction.

One thinks of Peter on the night the Lord Jesus was taken prisoner.

Someone told a story about one of her grandchildren that gives perspective on this matter. The girl was angry because her older brother set traps to catch birds. She cried when he wouldn't listen to her. Then she decided to do something specific about it. Shortly thereafter her mother noticed that the little girl was in a better mood and wanted to know what she had done about the problem.

"Well, first I prayed for Tom to be a better boy, and then I prayed that his trap wouldn't catch any more birds," the girl explained.

"Did that do it?" asked her mother.

"No. So then I went out and kicked the trap to pieces."

It takes a certain strength to pitch in and solve a problem as well as to passively endure. The whole point is that we need to be alert, conscious of the value of the well-ordered life, prepared in appropriate responses, and energetic about tackling it.

Life is not for sissies.

I knew that one more time when my husband and I were in a small private plane during a violent storm. The pilot was able, but we were being tossed above a section of high rocky mountains like a rampant kite, and there was nothing we could do about it. Six children would be left orphans if we didn't make it back. We prayed and we made it at last, but not before I had been thoroughly tried in faith and inner strength. It is one thing to write truth and platitudes, to speak and teach and believe God's principles for living and coping. It is quite another to be put to the test.

When this experience was all over, I thought about my out-of-control reactions. I was shocked that I seemed lacking in faith and so fearful. I was sick at heart that God might have forgotten us and the needs of those six children. I didn't want to accept that it might be "our time," like others whose names appear in the news after calamity. And I felt ashamed of my lack of strength.

Then began a new personal effort to become what a true believer must become.

The outpourings of grieving young Nephi were helpful. We'll include some of the thoughts here for your convenience now, but when you can you may want to study this reference for your own edification and comfort. Yes, comfort. It is like being allowed to read someone's private journal about his struggles and learnings. It is that personal. It is remarkable and helpful and relevant.

Nephi says that upon the plates he will write the things of his soul, and he will do this for the learning and profit of his children. And because he did, we who are down the generations can benefit, too.

He writes, "Nevertheless, notwithstanding the great goodness of the Lord, in showing me his great and marvelous works, my heart exclaimeth: O wretched man that I am! Yea, my heart sorroweth because of my flesh; my soul grieveth because of mine iniquities. I am encompassed about, because of the temptations and the sins which do so easily beset me. . . . Nevertheless, I know in whom I have trusted. My God hath been my support; he hath led me through mine afflictions in the wilderness; and he hath preserved me upon the waters of the great deep. He hath filled me with his love, even unto the consuming of my flesh. . . . He hath heard my cry by day, and he hath given me knowledge by visions in the nighttime. . . . If the Lord in his condescension unto the children of men hath visited men in so much mercy, why should my heart weep and my soul linger in the valley of sorrow, and my flesh waste away, and my strength slacken, because of mine afflictions? And why should I yield to sin, because of my flesh? Yea, why should I give way to temptations, that the evil one have place in my heart to destroy my peace and afflict my soul? Why am I angry because of mine enemy? Awake, my soul! No longer droop in sin. Rejoice, O my heart, and give place no more for the enemy of my soul. Do not anger again because of mine enemies. *Do not slacken my strength because of mine afflictions.* May the gates of hell be shut continually before me, because that my heart is broken and my spirit is contrite! . . . O Lord, I have trusted in thee, and I will trust in thee forever. . . . Yea, I know that God will give liberally to him that asketh.'' (2 Nephi 4:17–21, 23, 26–29, 32, 34, 35; italics added.)

There is not a word in that lament of Nephi's that cannot be eye-opening and soul-enlarging to us as we struggle under the burdens life imposes.

There is a choice line buried in a complicated letter from Paul to Timothy that has application: ''Thou therefore endure hardness, as a good soldier of Jesus Christ.''

And so we will. We'll be the good soldiers of Jesus Christ, come what may. But we had better learn how to do it sooner than later.

All around us are examples of common people doing uncommon things about the afflictions they are called upon to suffer. An especially attractive and talented young mother moved with her husband and little ones to a large metropolitan area while he completed schooling. She was able to continue developing her own unique talent in communication. Life held promise. Dreams could still come true if one worked hard enough—alone and together. That was their philosophy, at least.

They moved steadily in the direction of their dreams. Then, one day, the young mother was stricken with polio. Their world crashed around them. There was no one to take the little children. No money to ease the burden. Daddy's schedule had to be kept if he was to complete his medical training and not forfeit tuition and opportunities. Who was to hold the young mother's hand as she fought for her life—for their lives?

But God provided, and as events unfolded, it was the story of the Good Samaritan reenacted many times. Miracle upon miracle occurred it seemed. But it also was a story of the personal growth and great example of personal strength to others who needed it.

As the painful days passed and the mother healed, she began to share the gospel in her gifted, gentle way. She did it by explanation, by example, and by attitude. She did it by practical application of eternal principles when choices had to be made. And she witnessed humbly that clearly their own prayers were being answered. Affliction wasn't removed, but strength to deal with the problems did not slacken. God had lifted and blessed them.

Years later in a public setting, the woman expressed gratitude to Heavenly Father for this grim adventure with polio when she was a stranger in a big city. Without this experience she might never have learned precious truths so helpful to her in other situations down the years.

With all that you may be suffering now as one counted among the sick and afflicted, with all the heartbreak of physical deterioration, with all the unhappiness of love denied or dreams dashed or deprivation, now is the time to keep turning to God and to the word of God. Now is the time to experiment upon the principles of the gospel and prove whence cometh strength to overcome problems so you can move forward in inimitable joy!

There is no promise from God that we will be exempt from the very trials and experiences through which we can be forced to rely upon the Lord. Or dwindle in bitterness and unbelief. It isn't just overcoming sickness, bankruptcy, sin, or anything else on the long list of life's grim challenges. It is overcoming negative response to such things. We can either curse God and die, as Job was urged to do by his friends, or we can love God and with his help live above the trials.

Thinking back to President Brown, we wouldn't choose these trials, but in God's wisdom they come to us, and we find we are grateful to learn what we learn when our strength doesn't slacken in affliction.

14

Affliction
Be Praised

ituated at the edge of a field in a southern village was an open bower that had been turned into a church to accommodate the crowd. There was a large basket of freshly cut garden flowers next to the pulpit where the visiting preacher stood. He was silent for a few moments studying this country congregation. Some hung their heads and others looked about to each other. An observer would have noticed a certain discomfort among some of the worshippers.

Then there was a stir among the congregation as the preacher brushed aside a buzzing bee that alternately annoyed him and pollinated the flowers. At last he raised one hand in a kind of warning and said pontifically, "I have come to comfort the afflicted and afflict the comforted."

Small, nervous laughter sifted through the congregation. *They'd heard that before.*

Then this preacher carried out his twofold sermon by first rehearsing the fine promises the Lord has in store for His obedient children who endure (whatever and whatever!) to the end.

It had a salutary effect upon at least a portion of the congregation. After all, as any struggler can testify, affliction can push a person to his knees.

Second, the preacher pointed out the very real danger in complacency. Feeling comfort is . . . ah, well . . . comforting. Easy. However, unless the comforted watch and pray always, said this preacher, they can be easy prey for the adversary and his destructive cohorts.

Then the preacher reached for a rose and removed it from the bouquet to hold it before the people. He pointed to its exquisite petals and color. He described the inimitable fragrance. Sliding his fingers carefully down the tall stem, he revealed the thorns and said, ''The rose and thorn, the treasure and dragon, joy and sorrow all mingled into one'' (Saadi, *The Gulliston*, ch. vii Apologue xxi).

Like life.

Drawing heavily on the words of others now, the preacher drove home his point with a bit of truth whimsically phrased by Frank Stanton in his writing titled *This World*.

This world that we're a-livin' in
Is mighty hard to beat.
You git a thorn with every rose,
But *ain't* the roses *sweet!*

A summary of the preacher's message includes these important points that can be reminders for better living for us all:

Keep close to the Lord.
Be not comfortable nor complacent.
Expect trouble if you don't have it already.
Prepare for growth if you do—it's for your own good.
Count your blessings—it helps.
Be valiant—"there is no comfort for the wicked."

It is, after all, a very fine message. It is suitable for us as well.

Oh, how we'd rather be comfortable and complacent than afflicted with thorny experiences!

At best, if we must be counted among the afflicted, sick, and struggling for a time, most of us yearn for a hefty support system that plies us with compliments for our stoic behavior, that brings us our meals, lends us the money we need, cluck-clucks with us over the ill-treatment we have received from our creditors, and sympathizes tirelessly as we describe each new round in a family squabble.

(And it just might appropriately be added here that those who comfort are often afflicted by those whom they comfort!)

The important point is that you work your way through your problems, keeping very close to the Lord in the process.

Here are some familiar don'ts about keeping close to the Lord:

Don't forget to prepare your heart to commune with God.
Don't forget to pray.
Don't forget to stay awake while praying.
Don't forget to count your blessings.
Don't pray only for favors.
Don't pray for your own way instead of his will.

Don't forget to study the word of God so you will
know his will.
Don't forget to listen for the promptings.
Don't forget to repent.
Don't forget to be believing.
Don't forget to perform according to guidance re-
ceived.
Don't forget to love.

These familiar attitudes are practical and helpful when
one is among the sick and afflicted.

As you are going through a round of trial or suffering a
kind of real life nightmare, make a mental effort to increase
your patience. You really can't fully know God's will or his
timetable for you. Meanwhile, you may need to rehearse
again and again what you do know about the purpose of
life, as far as you understand it.

Being sick and afflicted is the time to shift gears immediately, to become thoughtful and meditative. Reassess
your values. Lessen the stressful aspects of the current situation by retreating out of the world—go to the temple,
find quiet time to ponder the word of God, to evaluate your
whole life and attitude at this critical point. And, stay on
your knees, literally and figuratively.

It is like going for the gold, isn't it? Training, preparedness, an attitude to win in a demanding situation separates
the gold medalists from the losers. Unlike participating in
the Olympics, each of us has a different race to run; we're
not in competition with anyone but ourselves. In spite of
afflictions we can be winners. With God nothing is impossible. It is worth the effort then to learn how to work with
God, how to get his help. Which is another way of saying
learning how to live by his commandments!

When trouble does come, spend at least as much time
finding a way to cope with it as grieving over it, worrying
about it, or writhing under it. Even search for a way to en-

dure it, to somehow flourish under it. One day you can look back in gratitude to God for lessons learned and progress made in strength of character. It is inevitable when these right steps are taken. Ask the person who has been through the process. What you know now, you couldn't possibly have understood in the same dimension without experience. Vicarious experiences are just not as compelling as the real affliction of suffering paralysis in your legs, the death of a loved one, a shattered reputation, anger toward a family member, or heartbreak in love, for example.

Now, by way of warning, if you are struggling mightily at this time, struggling and fighting because of broken health or demanding pressures, if you are sick and afflicted and therefore finding it ever so difficult to keep a sweet, faithful spirit, watch out! More than your physical life is at stake. I shiver when I read the lines of warning in 3 Nephi 18:15, 18: "Ye must watch and pray always, lest ye be tempted by the devil, and ye be led away captive by him. . . . for Satan desireth to have you, that he may sift you as wheat."

My interpretation is that Satan isn't going to fuss much with the poor souls who have given in already. He is engaged in war and is after the valiant warriors who are vulnerable to attack only if they remove themselves from their Leader. "Watch and pray always" our Leader has counseled. And here is the comfort in that same chapter Jesus promises that "whatsoever ye shall ask the Father in my name, *which is right, believing that ye shall receive,* behold it shall be given unto you."

If we were sitting about in a comfortable room discussing these sacred things together, surely there would not be one who couldn't witness that this is true. A search of one's life and soul will reveal the hand of God, the outpouring of his blessings that do come with our afflictions, not in spite of them. Afflictions be praised!

Because of my own sufferings, however small by comparison, my compassion has increased for Jesus. The Son of God—on the cross—felt the crush of being forgotten by the Father and cried out in anguish, "My God, why hast thou forsaken me?" Also, I ache for Joseph Smith—suffering greatly in Liberty Jail—who cried out to a Heavenly Father and the Lord *whom he had seen and talked to and been trained by for their work.* He was feeling forgotten and abandoned. Questioning. But he held on. He grew mightily and did some of his most vital work afterwards.

When we suffer afflictions, being left on our own for a time, we can remember that this, too, is obviously part of the test. The precedents are too compelling to assume otherwise. And we will not succumb to the depression the adversary imposes at such times. We will hold on! Stand! Wait! Know that ultimately such experience will be for our good as part of a loving Father's purpose.

Say it one more time to yourself. The gospel is true. It works. Christ lives. Heavenly Father feels for us more even than we feel for our offspring. We are not abandoned. We are simply given a chance to learn.

It was Henry Van Dyke who wrote, "The best rosebush, after all, is not that which has the fewest thorns, but that which bears the finest flowers."

Whatsoever state we find ourselves in, as we read in Philippians 4:11, we must strive "therewith to be content." Life requires it of us and rewards us for it.

Now, on to gather the rosebuds while we may.

15

Promises and
Pink Carnations

hen our neighbor Dorothy came to Church bravely wearing a corsage she'd made from her husband's funeral roses and gladioli, people were surprised. It was so soon.

Dorothy and Smitty had been a happily married young couple. For the teenagers in the neighborhood they were the ideal of a romantic marriage. They had several little children and a new home with a garden in back and chairs on the front porch to welcome the people who dropped in to visit the popular family.

Then Smitty's health began to fail, until finally heart surgery was performed—unsuccessfully. Now, only a day or two after the funeral, Dorothy stood in testimony meeting to declare her faith in God. She began by telling this little riddle:

Q. If all the people who were sick and afflicted were given a pink Cadillac, what kind of country would this be?

A. A pink carnation.

She explained that a little girl sitting there behind her in church had noticed that Dorothy was sad and tearful through the meeting. Her little girl's heart wanted to help. She thought of her favorite riddle and hoped it would brighten Dorothy's mood. She leaned forward across the church pew and whispered it to Dorothy.

It worked. That light approach gave Dorothy the moment she needed to shake the sadness, to stand with a smile, and speak of the promises she already had felt fulfilled from God. Even though Smitty no longer lived on earth, even though her prayers hadn't been answered the way she had hoped they would, she testified that she had been comforted, filled with peace from God that was real and powerful.

Dorothy told the congregation about the dear child who had shared the pink carnation story. She said, "I am grateful to God, too, for thoughtful people like my little friend, who was quick to see my need and try to be helpful in some way. It has helped me remember that we all can be instruments in the hands of God to bring forth His promises of solace and hope."

I never see a bouquet of pink carnations without being reminded of that sweet moment in a testimony meeting. For example, I went to the mortuary to support the parents of a three-month-old baby girl lying in a tiny casket with a bouquet of pink and white carnations resting on the top. This baby was the long-awaited joy of their hearts. There would be no more children in that family, and the mother's heart was broken. She struggled with her questions and her anger that her prayers had been ignored. She felt rejected by heaven. And it hurt.

I told the distraught mother about Dorothy and her little six-year-old friend a row back in church with the riddle of the pink carnations. She turned and fingered the lovely pink bouquet blanket over her beloved baby. She smiled at the simple humor and said, "Aren't children wonderful? They can restore our perspective in a hurry. Just knowing that people care about us in a time of sadness has a way of reminding us that surely God cares, as well."

And of course, he does.

So take heart if you are feeling forgotten. Take heart no matter how bad things seem for the moment.

There is a scripture that can make your day brighter because it carries a message of hope and promise. In the first verse of the ninety-eighth section of the Doctrine and Covenants the Lord reminds us, "Verily I say unto you [verily means *in truth*, you know] my friends, [he calls us his friends!] fear not, let your hearts be comforted; yea, rejoice evermore, and in everything give thanks; waiting patiently on the Lord, for your prayers have entered into the ears of the Lord of Sabaoth, and are recorded with this seal and testament—the Lord hath sworn and decreed [promised!] that they shall be granted."

You can't have a better promise than that.

We learn then that we should be comforted, that we are not forgotten, that we are Christ's friends, that he has heard our prayers, that we are to wait with patience, and that we shall be blessed. We also learn that God speaks the truth.

Many years ago President George Q. Cannon wrote on this subject, saying in part, "Though your prayers may not be answered immediately, if they are offered in the name of Jesus and in faith, nothing being left undone by you that is required, they will live on the records of Heaven and on the remembrance of the Lord and yet bear fruit'' (*Millennial Star*, vol. 25, pp. 74–75).

There is an impressive incident recorded in the Book of Mormon that shows that the Lord does keep his promises when people pour out their hearts to him and keep his commandments. Read Mosiah 24 for the full text.

> *The voice of the Lord came to them in their afflictions, saying:*
> *Lift up your heads and be of good comfort.*
> *I know of the covenant which ye have made unto me.*
> *I will covenant with my people and deliver them out of bondage.*
> *I will also ease the burdens which are put upon your shoulders.*
> *This I will do that ye may stand as witnesses for me hereafter.*
> *That ye may know of a surety that I, the Lord God, do visit my people in their afflictions.*

I have restated the promises God makes to us in that beautiful scripture. I did this so that as sufferers we will not forget the wonderful comfort that can come to us and what our part is in achieving it. This is an account of a people who were told they would be put to death by their government if they prayed to God. Still they prayed in their hearts, and God knew the thoughts of their hearts.

We worship, we can pray in public as well as private, we can hold prayer circles and put our names on prayer rolls without fear. We need to do these things in faith and on the first occasion of need as we remember God's promises and give him the opportunity to bless us.

I use that scripture in Mosiah every chance I get to remind myself and others of the plain truth about adversity, affliction, and God's ability to assuage our grief. Despair comes to people when they forget this.

But there is more to be learned from this scripture: "And now it came to pass that the burdens which were laid upon Alma and his brethren were made light." (*Their burdens were made light just as God had said they would be!*)

You see, for some reason problems aren't always resolved, nor can they be, exactly how and when we would have them. We know this. But if they can be made light, we can hang on. We will know of God's caring for us.

It reminds me of the time that I had coaxed my husband into going someplace against his will. I turned to him in the middle of the event and said, "Isn't this fun?" His dour reply has stood as a family joke all these years and says it well for us now. He said, "I came, didn't I? Do I have to have fun, too?"

We are to endure and be patient, and we're supposed to put on happy faces as well. The rest of that scriptural account is very interesting on this point. "Yea, the Lord did strengthen them that they could bear up their burdens with ease, and they did submit cheerfully and with patience to all the will of the Lord."

Now there is a stunner. We not only have to submit to affliction, but now we learn that we are expected to do it cheerfully. In other words, we are required to do more than merely hold on, gritting our teeth. We are to grin and bear whatever is plaguing us, trusting the Lord enough to act pleasant, patient, and accepting of our lot at the moment. If we acknowledge his help to us, we'll find we can be cheerful even in the midst of affliction.

The very determination to abide that counsel brings comfort. The Lord has told us repeatedly that when we are obedient, he is bound to reward us with blessings. What better comfort can there be than whatever the Lord gives us.

Let's say it one more time. Experiment upon the word.

1. *Count your blessings*

Name the good things God has given you, one by one. In our best moments, each of us can recall times when we have been comforted and strengthened by the Lord and times when our burdens have been eased, if not entirely removed. Let's give credit in such times of remembrance.

2. *Keep close to the Lord*

Often it takes a little time before we become converted to a principle, before habits and attitudes change and accommodate a better way. Meanwhile, draw ever closer to the Lord. Mentally, put your hand in his and feel him walking beside you over the rough way.

3. *Study the scriptures*

Over and over again we are reminded to find our answers and our direction, our solace and our strength, by scripture study. Why spin wheels in grief or anguish? Just do it! Comfort and ease does come.

4. *Be obedient*

Conscientiously apply gospel principles to problem solving and to spiritual survival when you are sick and afflicted. The Lord has said in many ways the thought, "I the Lord am bound when ye do what I say."

5. *Find a way to help others*

Everyone needs to understand this near-magic system for survival. When you learn, teach. When you feel you are a witness to God's goodness, testify of it to others. When you are sick or afflicted, reach out beyond yourself to help others. Give promises and pink carnations.

And now—what about that plea "O God, bless the sick and the afflicted"? He does. He does!

Index